CONTRIBUTIONS
TO MODERN EDUCATION

Founded by SUSAN ISAACS, M.A., D.SC.

Edited by EVELYN LAWRENCE

TESTING RESULTS
IN THE INFANT SCHOOL

CONTRIBUTIONS TO MODERN EDUCATION

Founded by SUSAN ISAACS, M.A., D.SC.
Edited by EVELYN LAWRENCE

Free Painting—Experimental School

TESTING RESULTS
IN THE INFANT SCHOOL

by

D. E. M. GARDNER, M.A.

HEAD OF THE DEPARTMENT OF CHILD DEVELOPMENT,
UNIVERSITY OF LONDON INSTITUTE OF EDUCATION

WITH 33 ILLUSTRATIONS

METHUEN & CO. LTD. LONDON
36 Essex Street, Strand, W.C.2

First published April 9th 1942
Second edition February 1948
Reprinted, with corrections, 1953

2.2

CATALOGUE NO. 3859/U

PRINTED IN GREAT BRITAIN BY
BUTLER & TANNER LTD., FROME AND LONDON

FOREWORD

HAVING had the privilege of following the early stages of Miss Gardner's inquiry into the tested effects of different modes of education in the Infant School, I awaited her final results with eager interest. And I will not deny that they surprised me—most agreeably!

My own and other people's experience had left no doubt that any such objective tests under proper conditions, comparing the achievements of children who were allowed to move and talk and play together with those who were mostly made to sit still and listen, would show solid and lasting gains by the former group *in many respects*. But it was far from certain that these gains would be enough to count, or would even appear, in all directions. It was quite possible that children taught on narrower and more formal lines would get ahead more rapidly in certain respects than those whose broader interests and natural modes of learning were given scope. We knew that children allowed to be active and companionable would prove more lively and inquiring, more inventive and enterprising, more resourceful and co-operative than the others. But no one could say *how much more*. And it might be true that those who were persuaded to toe the line would appear to do better in those subjects of formal learning by which the Infant School still so commonly seeks to justify itself.

It is so easy, when attempting to form opinions by simple observation or impressionistic comparisons, to fall into the snare of comparing the best schools with the worst, the best of those which adopt one method with the worst of those which follow another (and this would work either way according to one's prejudices). It was obviously essential that the results of the two educational methods should be studied with children of the same range of intelligence and similar homes and social backgrounds. In any case, there is a world of difference between general impressions and probabilities and the precise knowledge of measured facts, facts which have been gathered under objective conditions, and with all the proper safeguards of a sound technique of testing and of evaluating data.

Miss Gardner's modesty and reserve in presenting her general conclusions are as evident as her care in preparing the experimental conditions, her ingenuity in devising her tests and her good judgment in applying them.

Her actual results, set forth in Chapters III to VI, and summarized on pp. 144–5, are clear and unequivocal. They show that not even in those matters which they would claim as their own special virtues are the schools were children sit still and listen superior to those where children move and talk and play. The former group do no better in the three R's, or in carrying out a task in handwork neatly and carefully. They are less successful in concentrating on a task which they are asked to do but which is not immediately interesting, and in written compositions (at eight years of age).

I will leave Miss Gardner's pages to tell their own further story. They will convince doubting Thomas. They will encourage and support all those understanding teachers who have long struggled against half-hearted authorities, or battled with adverse buildings and meagre equipment, to meet the true needs of children in the Infant School.

SUSAN ISAACS

Cambridge
December 1941

PREFACE

I WISH to express my warm thanks to Dr. Ll. Wynn Jones, of the University of Leeds, for his help throughout this research and for the time he so generously spent on calculating the significance of my results, and also to Miss Newcomb, M.A., for sympathetic advice when I have consulted her about this work.

I also thank Dr. Susan Isaacs for a great deal of most valuable advice, and for her warm interest in this work throughout the three years while I was devising and giving tests, as well as in preparing the book for publication.

Among the very many people to whom I am much indebted I wish to mention Dr. Mary MacTaggart and Dr. Schonell for help and advice with the tests in reading and arithmetic; Miss Gwen Chesters and many friends and colleagues who have acted as assessors of results of various tests; Miss Alice Stephen, who undertook the tests in physical training; and my old student, Elizabeth Jenkinson, who gave laborious days to helping me administer and mark the tests, and whose skill with the children and carefully recorded observations have been of the greatest possible assistance.

I also acknowledge gratefully the kindness of the Education Authorities of Leeds, Wakefield, and the West Riding, and the Head Teachers and staff of more than twenty schools, who, despite very difficult conditions at times, never failed to give me every facility for carrying out tests.

Owing to the present shortage of paper and the increased cost of publication, I have found it necessary to omit the tables containing the scores of individual children in the tests. The significance of the result of each test is given, and also the method of calculating the significance, from which it can be seen that no test is claimed to be significant merely on the grounds that a few children's scores are very much higher in one school than in another. Results designated 'significant' are those in which the superiority of children in one school over another is marked in a large number of cases.

Other material which has been omitted is: (1) the tests in arithmetic, since such tests are easy to obtain or devise; (2) an analysis of the scores of twenty-two children in the Pintner-Cunningham, and forty-eight children in the Alexander test; and (3) a short description of tests which I began to use, but was forced to abandon owing to war-time difficulties.

The full tables of results or any of the above material can be supplied to any research worker who may care to go into them, but for the general reader they are outside the main purpose of this book, and have been omitted in the interests of economy.

Fig. 1 is reproduced from *Billy Bobtail*, by Alec Buckels, by courtesy of Messrs. Faber and Faber.

D. E. M. G.

January 1942

NOTE TO SECOND EDITION

SINCE the first edition of this book I have begun to give more advanced tests to children of nine years with the object of discovering the longer distance effects of the two types of Infant School education. My results are not yet complete, though it is hoped to publish them later. Another investigator has, however, obtained some results in Arithmetic with children aged nine years who at an earlier age were subjects in my research. These results are given on page 134.

D. E. M. G.

August 1947

CONTENTS

PLATES

CHAPTER I

TWO TYPES OF INFANT SCHOOLS: THE NEED TO STUDY COMPARATIVE RESULTS

LET US imagine that you are visiting two schools, each very good of its kind and staffed by efficient and interested teachers, but using very different methods based upon an important difference of principle.

[1]When you enter the first school, 'A', you find the hall full of children. One characteristic of this school is that the teachers are greedy for space, and use every bit they have to its best advantage. You will hear busy, interested children's voices—'Move that barrow, then we can build this line right round'—'Can I have some of your red paint?'—'Why don't you put a propeller on your aeroplane?' There are the children—building, hammering, sliding, washing; you will have to search for the teacher—she will at first be scarcely visible among her class of forty or more. When you discover her, perhaps she is holding John's nail while he bangs, because every one else is busy and he cannot quite manage on his own; and at the same time, she is turning round to call, 'Mary, that doll does look comfortable, you have made that bed well —everything in the right place'; 'Yes, Ian, the screws are in my cupboard, bottom shelf'; and so on and so forth.

Besides this set of children using the hall, there will be others passing through on all sorts of errands to do with their own affairs. These will be walking, dawdling, running, skipping, according to temperament, but all quite clear about where they are going and why.

You may meet in the corridors a whole class going out to play with brightly coloured balls, ropes, hoops, etc. They will probably be on one side of the corridor, if its width makes

[1] For this description of the schools I am indebted to Elizabeth Jenkinson, who visited them frequently and has recorded the vivid impressions which they made upon her as an interested 'outsider'.

that the sensible thing to do; but they will certainly be walking along easily, in twos and threes, chattering.

If you look through the windows or possibly the open doors of the classrooms, you will see children standing before easels or sitting on the floor painting on large papers with fat brushes, putting dolls to bed, scrubbing tables, polishing handles, moulding clay, making sand-pies, measuring water, hammering wood, serving in shops, sewing stage clothes, building bricks, doing sums, reading to themselves, to each other, or the teacher, writing letters to invite the children in the next class to a play performance, or occupied in many similar pursuits.

A child may be folding up, in order to take home, a very attractive drawing, while one not nearly as good is being pinned on the wall by the teacher as the painter looks on proudly. Another may be writing very carefully and not very tidily the word 'buttercup', which he will then put before a jar so that all may know and recognize the contents, while he sets about finding how to spell and write 'daisy'; whereas a really beautifully written, 'Dear Alan, our rabbit has had some babies. What shall we feed them on?' goes into the recipient's pocket and is never seen again.

Some children sit still some of the time, some sit still none of the time, none sit still most of the time. This recognized right to move about freely means that space is needed; so in these classrooms there is nothing except the things the children need and use, whilst tables and chairs are moved without fuss as and when required. Pictures are hung so that people three feet high can look at and touch them; shelves are low, so that they can fetch and carry the things they need. In short, the school is a child-sized world for children to move and learn in.

The impression made on you cannot fail to be one of purpose. All these children know what they want to do and how to set about it. You get a sense of poise which is confirmed when you ask the way to the headmistress, for as you are taken to her you will almost certainly be entertained by friendly conversation and much information, of a kind which is only given when a child's relations with grown-ups are easy and serene.

Now let us go to the second school, 'B'.

The very first thing you notice, when you go into the hall, is the quiet; no talking, laughing, shouting; at most, a chant from a whole class, reciting a poem or a table. The second thing is the absence of children. Where are they? If there are any in the hall, and there well may not be, since such schools do not need space so urgently—they will be in one group, doing the same thing, and the teacher will be in front of them, striving by word, action, and suggestion, with a very high degree of skill and energy, to influence the forty children before her in the direction she thinks desirable.

Through this hall there will be no stream of purposeful children, but at most an occasional one or two, very probably on some errand for their teacher.

If you meet a class going out, the children will probably have the same attractive-looking apparatus, but they will certainly be in a straight line, and very probably not talking.

As you look through the windows of the other classrooms your first impression cannot fail to be of 'desks' (you will automatically think of them as 'desks', though they may in fact be tables), then of a teacher, and finally of children in the desks. There they will be, children of all ranges of intelligence and temperament, doing sums, or painting, or plasticene or paper-cutting; doing several rather interesting kinds of things, but the members of each class doing the same thing at the same time. The children hardly ever exchange ideas with each other as they work, since in such schools creative thinking is not as important as acquiring skills, such as neat cutting-out, good writing, etc. Talking whilst practising these skills would waste time. It is, therefore, not approved and often, for long periods, is not allowed.

As you pass you will see many lessons given which from the technical point of view are excellent. Many attractive materials will be used. You will not be able to doubt that the teachers are efficient and well-disposed towards the children. But look at the groups of children and see if there is one class, whatever its activity, in which *every* child is interested and using his powers for that activity to his fullest extent!

Also ask yourself if it is likely that this simultaneous interest of a whole class could be aroused by one woman not once, as a result of superb determination, but every day, several times.

You will find your doubts confirmed by the fact that the teacher agrees that the best work always comes from the same relatively small set of children; and you will notice that the drawing, writing, and sums put up on the wall are all 'best' work.

In one class a boy will move from his place. This will be very obvious in a room where every one else is sitting, so comment and inquiry will be made, and unless the child's reason is very good the move will certainly be disapproved. This is not ill-will on the part of the teacher, but a perfectly consistent outcome of the accepted theory. Where skills are imparted directly from teacher to pupil it is necessary that the pupil shall be under the constant and immediate control of the teacher.

You will notice a considerable amount of fidgeting. At regular intervals, rarely more often than once a day, the need for the children to move is recognized by periods for physical training and dancing. It is also informally recognized sometimes by the teacher saying in the middle of a lesson, 'All stand up—stretch—jump high—touch your toes—sit down.' But the very large majority of the children's time, as you can see from studying their time-table, is spent sitting down.

You will find a far greater number of 'naughty' children in this school. This, again, need not show any ill-will towards the children; it is another quite consistent result of the method, which does not allow for a child's most natural means of expression; talking, touching, moving. All these necessarily become undesirable except when they coincide with the teacher's purposes. If you should point this out to the teachers they will probably reply, 'There is a time and place for everything. Of course they can do these things at the proper time.' Or, 'It is good for them to learn to sit still, to be quiet, not to touch.' You will have hit on some attitudes fundamentally different from those in the other school, where the teachers would say, 'It is only good for children to do these things for a purpose which they appreciate. To sit still so that they can be counted, to be quiet because the new boy has hurt his head, not to touch the rabbit any more because it would like a rest,' for example.

A facet of the relationship between teacher and child in this school is the practice of 'Hands up'. This is necessary where the limits set to a child's movements mean that he cannot simply go up to the teacher and talk to her, but needs and ought to have some means of attracting her attention. So he puts up his hand. This very often comes to be connected in his mind with school and authority, so that should an outsider go into such a school to teach, test, or call the register, and address a child directly, he will, while answering, put up and often keep up his hand.

Note the response in this school when you ask the way to the headmistress. Your question will be answered; but it is unlikely that any extra information will be volunteered, unless you have met one of the school's bright children. You will feel in the child's manner either a complete refusal to make a contact with you, or a certain keenness to estimate what sort of behaviour you want from him and to behave that way. You will conclude that he is a little tense, a little anxious, in his contact with grown-ups.

These schools show such very different pictures because they live out no less different theories of child nature and education.

Both sets of teachers would agree that they would like their children to be happy and sociable, and as intellectually skilled as their intelligence makes possible. The difference of method is due to the fact that the first school accepts the children's impulses to learn through doing and works through these towards its object, whilst the second school ignores these impulses, super-imposes upon them the teacher's purposes, or uses them in the teacher's time and way, not the children's. With so much in common in their aims, both sets of teachers should welcome a critical examination of the results of their method.

DIFFERENT VIEWS OF THE CHILD'S NATURE AND NEEDS

School 'B' is a product of the belief that the young child is a helpless being, very much in need of our direction if he is to learn the skills which will fit him to take his place in our complex society. The teacher therefore is envisaged chiefly as an instructor whose first duty is to maintain order, so that the pupils may be in a suitable condition to receive instruction. She will, if she is a good teacher, be able to maintain order by kindly means, but she has no doubt that her duty is to mould her pupils in the way which she believes to be most desirable for their future welfare. She is sure that the teacher knows better than the child what knowledge and skills he should have at each stage of his development and she will impart these to him by the best teaching technique and devices at her command.

School 'A', on the other hand, is an expression of the belief that the child contains in himself the germs of future goodness and perhaps greatness, and that the purpose of education is to foster growth. The teacher believes that a child provided with an environment varied in content and rich in creative possibilities and watched sympathetically by understanding and skilled teachers will select, at the time when he is ready for it, material through which he can acquire the knowledge and experience he needs.

She believes that her chief function is to watch and provide for the harmonious expansion of the child's powers. She is ready to help him to acquire knowledge and skill, but only as his awakening curiosity and desires lead him to feel the need for them.

To such a teacher the child's spontaneous play is of great importance, and to foster it is one of her chief objects.

THE CHILD'S PLAY AS A MEANS OF EDUCATION

The present situation in Infant School education is one of great interest. I have myself witnessed, in the last twenty years, a steady growth in the acceptance by Infant School teachers of principles which, whilst not indeed new, were far from widely applied in the Elementary Infant Schools of twenty or even ten years ago. They are still to-day often challenged and even when accepted are yet not fully applied in a large number of Infant Schools.

The principle of educating young children through their spontaneous activity or play is, however, by no means a product of recent times.

Greek education, for instance, recognized the value of children's tendency to play. Plato says in the Seventh Book of *Laws*, 'At three, four, five and six years the childish nature will require play. Children at that age have certain natural modes of amusement which they find out for themselves when they meet. And all children who are between the ages of three and six ought to meet . . . the several families of a village uniting on one spot and the nurses seeing to the children behaving properly . . .'

In the *Republic* also he refers several times to the value of play.

It is impossible in the scope of this book to summarize the recognition of play in the history of education, but both ideas that play is of value in education and that it is inimical, have a long history. Among the advocates of play have been Vittorino da Feltre, Locke, Rousseau, Pestalozzi, Basedow, Richter, and Froebel.

Froebel particularly exerted a strong influence in this country, and although for a time the unfortunate concentration on his 'Gifts and Occupations' imposed a formality on children's play which Froebel never intended, these were gradually discarded and his great principle of 'self activity' began to obtain recognition. In the early days of the Infant School in this country, Robert Owen and to a somewhat lesser degree Samuel Wilderspin both recognized the value of play. The strongest influence on the schools to-day in the direction of education through play is perhaps Professor John Dewey's. He insists on the importance of allowing young children to observe the world around them and to learn by unorganized experience. Dewey's work has influenced the education not only of children in the Infant School, but of older children also, for the project method is an extension of the play principle to the interests and natural pursuits of older children.

The Report of the Consultative Committee of the Board of Education in 1933 on Infant and Nursery Schools shows clearly that the principle of education based on play is accepted by the authors of the Report. The principle is both directly stated, as (on page 125), 'During the Infant Stage the play way is the best way,' and indirectly implied by advocating playgrounds and gardens, toys and equipment which will encourage play.

The 1937 *Handbook of Suggestions* also refers to the value of play and group activities in the Infant School, as well as in the Nursery School or class.[1]

Psychologists are almost unanimous in advocating play, often in emphatic terms. The various theories of play, too well known to require expansion in the limited space of this study, all emphasize one or more aspects of the value of play. It is advocated as a preparation for life, as an outlet for surplus energy or for strong primitive emotions which are denied expression in our socialized environment, as rest and recreation, as an opportunity to acquire rapidly experiences which the race took thousands of years to undergo, as fulfilling biological needs by promoting growth, as providing compensations for difficulties and frustrations in the individual personality, as leading to self-realization and so to character development, and as an incentive to the acquisition of knowledge.

Among the leading psychologists in the field of child development, the value of play is put forward in the strongest terms. Susan Isaacs refers many times to its value in promoting learning and in stabilizing the child's emotional life, as well as to its function of helping him to understand the complexities of social relationships. Charlotte Bühler, William Stern, Louisa Wagoner, and many other psychologists whose work

[1] *Handbook of Suggestions for Teachers.* Board of Education, 1937, pages 81 and 82.

is concerned with young children also have much to say of play as an educative influence.[1]

To illustrate the acceptance of the value of play, the following paragraph from a modern text-book in psychology[2] will serve:

'In their play children learn to observe quickly, to judge, to weigh values, to pick out essentials, to give close attention; they learn the value of co-operation, to recognise the rights of others as well as to insist on their own being recognised; they learn the value of freedom through law; they learn the value and function of work and the joy of accomplishment. No wonder that play is regarded by many as the most important educational factor of them all.' Such statements in varying degrees of clarity and emphasis are to be found in most of the text-books of educational psychology which are in the hands of Infant School teachers.

In fact the principle that young children are best educated by means of their play is very generally accepted by educationists in this country and in America. In practice, however, there is a wide divergence in the procedure adopted in various Infant Schools. Some schools, still in a minority, carry out fully the principle of education through play or 'self activity'. Others follow a very different practice. The general public, as a whole, is even less convinced than the educational world about the value of play in school. It is possible to trace the idea that play is trivial or even harmful back to early beliefs. Play was viewed with suspicion in the early Christian era, and found little place in the schools of the Renaissance period. In the early days of Elementary education in this country it was perhaps natural that the necessity of teaching the illiterate masses to read should occupy the foremost place in the minds of those concerned with education, and that despite the influence of such men as Robert Owen, the temptation to press formal instruction on very young children should creep into the schools, a temptation which was greatly increased

[1] Books on the value of play are referred to in Sections I and II of the bibliography.

[2] *The Psychology of Childhood.* Norsworthy and Whitley, 1937, p. 131.

when the system of 'payment by results' was instituted. Under this system play was inevitably looked upon as a waste of school time, and this attitude has not entirely vanished from the minds of many teachers.

Moreover, apart from any question of tradition, there are undoubtedly many people who become disturbed and anxious at the sight of young children engaged in play in school. They expect mischief and trouble to arise when the children's activities are not directed by a teacher, and they fear that children educated in this way will grow up without knowledge or self-control. They are quick to trace disturbances in the world and social behaviour of which they disapprove to the excessive freedom which they allege is given in schools to-day. There is often tolerance of play as recreation, but not as an integral part of the educational system.

Teachers in the schools which use play as a means of education have frequently to reassure parents and try to convince them that their children are really receiving education as well as enjoying themselves, and they often have to meet criticism of their methods from the teachers in the upper schools. Moreover, it requires more skill and intelligence to educate children through their spontaneous activity than to follow more formal and prescribed systems of instruction, and it is more difficult to assess the value of the result obtained. The enthusiasm with which the Montessori system was embraced by many teachers was probably due to the fact that it offered the security of a prescribed series of activities with an exact procedure determined beforehand, while at the same time it allowed for freedom of movement and apparent informality for the children. In Infant Schools which do not base their education on play, there is a genuine desire on the part of many teachers to make school life happy and attractive for the children, and if the teachers were convinced that the children would really benefit from more play in school they would give it. From their point of view as much as from the point of view of teachers who use the methods based on play, it would be of great value if many skilled investigators would take up the task of measuring the results, including the long-distance results, of these different types of education. At present there are many theories both for and against education based on play, but there has been very little exact and unbiassed investigation of the question.

THE PURPOSE OF THIS RESEARCH

The chief purpose of this research was, thus, to investigate some of the results of the different types of education given in public Elementary Infant Schools to-day.

If the effect upon the development and the school achievement of children, over a space of years, of the different methods now in use could be fully established on a scientific basis, it would serve the cause of education in many ways.

It would give the teachers and those who train them a sense of solid security about the value of methods which are now often followed in a spirit of faith rather than of knowledge, or rejected because the result is felt to be uncertain and dangerous. It would lead to the rejection of bad and the firmer establishment of good methods. It would provide a standard against which the effects of new methods and further development in educational practice could be measured.

The present investigation is only a small beginning in a field which is very wide. Fully satisfactory results could only be obtained by many workers using many tests and with large numbers of children and schools.

For such a research tests would need to be standardized. Except in reading and arithmetic, there are at present very few standardized tests for measuring the attainments of children of six, seven, and eight years. Nor apart from the tests of intelligence are there many tests for measuring those qualities and attitudes towards life and school work which it is the aim of most Infant Schools to produce. Few teachers would assert that a measurement of the capacity of six and seven-year-olds to read and work sums gives an adequate picture of the results of Infant School education. Moreover, tests designed to measure innate intelligence must of their very nature be unsuitable for measuring the results of education.

A subordinate purpose to my main one, but closely bound up with it, was to attempt to work out a procedure for testing certain qualities and attainments in young children for which there are at present few or no standardized tests. If any later investigators should be willing to use any of these tests, and hence improve upon them or confirm them, I should consider that this investigation had been worth while for that reason alone.

I decided to confine my own investigation to the education of children aged five to eight years, because there is much more divergence of opinion about this field of education than about that of children under five. Most Nursery Schools and classes in England nowadays educate the children under five largely by means of play, although in some cases routine and toilet training, music, sense training, and speech training occupy a very large part of the day, and in some schools the four-year-olds have considerably less play than the three-year-olds. On the whole, however, the principle of education by means of play is both accepted and applied in the education of children under five, but at five years old the children in many schools begin their formal education, and play is reduced to a very subordinate position if it is included at all in their curriculum. In the good schools of the more formal type, the time is largely spent in the presentation by the teacher of instruction carefully and logically planned in graded steps, and in the practice by the children of activities and exercises designed to impress this instruction on their minds.

In the Bibliography (Section I) I have referred to books which describe good schools of the type in which education is based on play and which illustrate the kind of methods used in the 'experimental' schools of this study.

I decided to choose pairs of schools in different types of social district, one of which was a good school in which education was based on play or spontaneous activity, and the other a good school of the formal type. I excluded any of the latter in which the teaching was very narrow or the children were unhappy. Having paired the children according to age, sex, and intelligence, I purposed to test them as widely as possible for those qualities and attainments which it is the generally accepted aim of Infant education to encourage.

PREVIOUS STUDIES

To many other investigators I am indebted for ideas which proved indirectly helpful in this research. I have referred to these briefly under the heading 'Further Acknowledgments', at the end of this book.

Very little work has been done on the actual subject of this inquiry. Jones and Burks in a survey published in 1936, of methods and experimental findings on personality development in childhood[1] state, 'Data have been singularly lacking which would permit any clear evaluation of the outcomes of "progressive" education as compared with "conventional" education, particularly in terms of the personality traits of the pupils.' They refer to 'A straw of evidence upon this problem' which is contained in Hartshorne and May's *Studies in Deceit.*[2] In the course of this study it was found that there was significantly less cheating among the pupils of an experimental progressive school than among those of a conventional school 'drawing their pupils from approximately the same socio-economic stratum'.

Considerably less research has been done on the psychology of children aged six to nine years than on either younger or older children. The statement made when the Board of Education's Report on 'The Primary School' was published in 1931 is still on the whole true: 'The data for a comprehensive psychological description of the period between the ages of seven and eleven are at present very imperfect: . . . much work has been recently done on the periods of earlier and later infancy; but no psychologist has hitherto concentrated specifically on the characteristics of the growing boy or girl from the age of seven to the onset of puberty.'[3] It would be as true to say 'from the age of six'. Much research has taken place since 1931, but it is still the pre-school child who has attracted

[1] *Personality Development in Childhood.* Jones and Burks, 1936, p. 110.
[2] *Studies in Deceit.* Hartshorne and May, 1928.
[3] *The Primary School.* Board of Education, 1931, p. 33.

much greater attention than the child of six or seven years old. Doubtless this is partly due, especially in America, to the increase of Nursery Schools and to the very good facilities which these offer for observing the young child under conditions of comparative freedom, as well as to the very spontaneous nature of the young child's behaviour which naturally attracts the student of psychology. In America the 'school age' does not begin until six, so there are many researches which include five-year-old children. There is a less severe gap between these researches and my own than between researches on four-year-old subjects and mine, but development is very rapid between five and six or seven, and the same technique for testing will not always apply.

Researches on children at other ages have, however, often proved suggestive to me in choosing and assessing the tests for this research.

CHOICE OF SCHOOLS : SOCIAL BACKGROUND

The first task was to select the schools to be used as experimental and control schools.

In order to avoid the danger of testing the effects of the Infant School education upon children from one particular type of home only, it was decided to choose schools in districts differing as widely as possible in social prosperity. Since the parents nearly always send their children to the infant school nearest to their homes, the children may fairly be described as a random sample of those who live in a certain neighbourhood.

Six experimental schools (called 'A' in this study) were first sought out. It was determined to use more schools than was strictly necessary to represent the different districts, because of the likelihood that during the three years required for the experiments, certain schools would fall out. This proved to be the case and unfortunately it was the two schools at the extreme ends of the social scale which could not be used for the final experiment. School (i)A was closed owing to the demolition of bad houses in the district.

School VA was in a very prosperous area, and many of the children went on from the Infant or Junior Schools to Secondary Schools. Details of reorganization within the school meant that the children at six and a half years of age were not under the 'experimental' conditions in the second year. The remaining schools, IA, IIA, IIIA, and IVA, represent ascending order of social district, school IA being in nearly as poor an area as school (i)A, and school IVA being in a district where the children come from comfortable homes. Two control schools (called 'B' throughout this study) were then selected to compare with each of the experimental schools. There were more schools of the 'B' type from which to choose. This meant that eighteen schools had to be used in the first year, but rendered it unlikely that experimental schools would have to be lost through the loss of control schools. Actually two of the control schools fell out through changes in the policy of teachers during the three years. In no case was any school lost through the unwillingness of teachers to co-operate. They were unfailingly courteous and co-operative, even though they were not told the purpose of the tests.

The social status of the parents of children in the various schools used for the experiment may be approximately seen from the types of occupation most common among them.

*School I*A. Unemployment very common. Casual labour. Most of those employed are labourers. A few small shopkeepers and better-paid occupations.

*School I*B. Slightly more prosperous socially than IA, but also very poor. Several fathers unemployed and other homes described by the Head Teacher as 'very poor' or 'rough'. Several manual labourers, but more fathers in better paid employment than in School IA.

*School II*A. A mixed district. Several unemployed. Several casual labourers. A good deal of distress, desertions, and some crime among the parents. Others in quite comfortable circumstances. Small shopkeepers, caretakers, travellers, plumbers, electricians, tram-drivers, and workers in a tailoring factory.

*School II*B. Very much like IIA, the home conditions ranging from quite severe poverty in a fairly large proportion of cases

3

to quite comfortable circumstances where the father is in regular work.

*School III*A. Little unemployment, but a few poor families. The majority, however, are comfortably situated. Several own their own small businesses. Some are commercial travellers, motor engineers, one a chemist, and some teachers. Some are van-drivers and one a dustman. Most children, but not quite all, are well dressed and healthy-looking.

*School III*B. A little poverty, but in some cases these poorer children are as well cared for as the others. Parents' occupations vary a good deal. Some are clerks, shopkeepers, teachers, policemen, asylum attendants, railwaymen. Others are miners and labourers.

*School IV*A. The children come from good working-class homes, not any more prosperous than the best homes in School IIIA, but without the group of poorer children that IIIA contains. Some of the fathers own their own businesses or are managers of firms. Others, the majority, work in local industries, iron and steel, clothing, printing, building, leather, and tailoring. The children are well fed and clothed, and well cared for generally.

*School IV*B. This school is situated very near School IVA, and the parents are employed in much the same occupations. Other occupations mentioned by the Head Teacher are: cabinet-making, furniture removing, foundry work, and first aid post. The children are well dressed and well cared for. There is practically no poverty.

In Schools VA and VB the parents are nearly all engaged in clerical and professional occupations, and a few are in trade. These children are extremely well cared for and have been taken about the country a good deal. They have plenty of books and toys at home.

THE CHARACTERISTICS OF AN EXPERIMENTAL SCHOOL

The essential characteristic of an experimental school for the purpose of this research is that it is one in which the children acquire a great deal of their education by means of their own spontaneous activity, watched over, and to a certain extent guided, by the teachers. The guidance does not consist of interference with the child's play nor in teaching him how to play, but in providing the materials and conditions which will best help him to carry out his own purposes and satisfy his own desire to learn. The teacher also discusses his plans with him in such a way as will help him to clarify his purposes, and gives him any information for which he may be seeking. She exercises her authority if necessary to prevent accidents or injuries to any child or to toys or apparatus.

In all these schools a period of at least $1\frac{1}{2}$ hours daily (and usually considerably more) when the child is under six, and at least an hour when he is over six, is devoted to spontaneous 'play activities'. Apart from this set time, the general approach to knowledge in most of the subjects of the curriculum is made by means of the children's spontaneous activity. For instance, they study nature by gardening, by arranging flowers and caring for pets rather than by formal nature lessons. The 'conversation lesson' is replaced by spontaneous talk with the teacher and between the children whilst activities of many kinds are in progress. In handwork lessons the child's purposes are considered rather than exercises in acquiring certain types of manual skill. In art lessons the child paints from his imagination the pictures he wants to paint, instead of drawing from models or learning formal pattern and design.

In reading, writing, and arithmetic the first approach is made by providing materials and experiences which will stimulate the child's desire to learn these subjects. Before reading is actually taught, attractive books, notices, and labels are placed in the classroom and the children attempt to read them and often ask for help. Writing is generally first introduced by helping the child to label his drawing or his own possessions or to write a message that he wants to send. Number is introduced by playing at shops, and by many games and materials for play which involve scoring and counting.

By the time the children are six, a set time daily is given in all the schools to the teaching of reading, writing, and arithmetic. In some cases, especially of more backward children the teachers would prefer to postpone this teaching,[1] but in view of the need to promote the child at seven (or soon after) to the Junior School, they consider it inadvisable to do this. Although a certain amount of drilling and practising is taken in the periods devoted to 'formal work' in reading, writing, and arithmetic, the possibility of using the child's purposes whenever possible and of keeping his curiosity alive is borne in mind. Very little, if any, systematic teaching of reading and arithmetic is given before the children are six or nearly six.

The actual times devoted by the experimental schools to 'play activities', and to practice work in reading, writing, and arithmetic each week is shown below.

5–6 years old	Play Activities	Systematic Teaching of Reading, Writing, and Arithmetic
School IA.	8 hrs. 20 mins.	2½ hours of very informal work
IIA.	17½ hours per week	0
IIIA.	13½ ,, ,, ,,	0
IVA.	8¼ ,, ,, ,,	0

6–7 years old		
School IA.	6 hours per week	7½ hours
IIA.	8 ,, ,, ,,	7 ,,
IIIA.	5 ,, ,, ,,	7½ ,,
IVA.	6 ,, ,, ,,	5 ,,

During the first year of this study an inquiry was made into the nature of the toys and materials for play provided in the various experimental schools. If a school was short of any important type of material, its use was suggested, and in some cases provided. In all the schools, however, many of the materials in each of the following groups were already in use.[2]

I

Toys mainly for functional activity and for the younger and less developed children.

[1] This point of view was expressed particularly in the case of School IIA.
[2] This list had been drawn up by a local Inspector and was available for consultation by interested teachers.

Toys to pull, push, and ride, e.g.
Tricycles, wagons, barrows, etc., prams, funboat, swing, hobby horse, hoops, etc., rocking horse.

To climb
Jungle gym., boxes, ropes, etc.

To manipulate
Water (with measures, spoons, funnels, and floating objects), sand trays, clay, dough, beads, bricks, paper, etc.

II

Materials productive of activity in older and more developed children.

Manipulative
Fitting toys, nest of boxes, etc., jig-saws, bricks and blocks, water, sand (wet), clay, dough, paper, wood, cloth, etc.

Constructional
'Tinker Toy', 'Edifex', 'Matador', 'Meccano', etc.

III

For imaginative and dramatic play
  (i) Dolls and all accessories, clothes, beds, houses, tea-sets, prams.
 (ii) For household play: laundry, cookery and sweeping sets, play-house.
(iii) Neighbourhood life: toy animals, vehicles, boats, trains, stations, shops, garages, cranes, windmills, aeroplanes.
(iv) Clothes and properties for 'dressing up'.

Materials for expression
Paper, pencil, crayons, paints, cloth, needles, thread, wood, hammers, nails, saws, etc.

V

Games
Balls, bats, quoits, skittles, marbles, etc.

Table Games
Dominoes, cards, happy families, snap, dice, snakes and ladders, ludo, etc.

VI

For the satisfaction of scientific curiosity

Scales and balances, magnets, prisms, lenses, humming tops and colour tops, etc.

VII

Miscellaneous materials collected and used by the children.

Empty boxes, tins, bottles, spools, string, wire, corks, buttons, household utensils.

THE CHARACTERISTICS OF A 'CONTROL' SCHOOL

A control school for the purpose of this research is a school in which the children are taught mainly by means of activity directed or knowledge presented by the teacher. The teacher plans her instruction according to a formal scheme which will lead the children step by step to the acquisition of the knowledge and skill which she intends them to acquire. Care was taken to avoid choosing schools in which the discipline was very repressive. It is obviously impossible to have as much freedom in a school of this kind as in one where spontaneous activity is the keynote of the education given, but the schools used are not those in which children as a whole are unhappy or frightened. Nor are they schools with a very narrow curriculum. Reading, writing, and arithmetic are considered the most important subjects, and considerably more time is spent on them than in the experimental schools and they are taught earlier, but they are not the only subjects taught. All subjects, however, are directed by the purposes of the teacher rather than by those of the child himself, although efforts are often made to win his co-operation and he is encouraged chiefly by means of praise or exhortation to improve his work. He often takes a pleasure in winning approval and may work with zest. Except for a special treat sometimes on a Friday afternoon, periods of 'play activities' do not occur on the time-table, and the teacher does not consider such periods to be of serious educational value, but rather as recreative. It is difficult to collect exact data about the times given to formal instruction because the terminology differs in the different schools, but the time devoted to reading, writing, and arithmetic in the school which probably spends the least time on this work is $1\frac{1}{2}$ hours each day with the children of five to six, and 2 hours with the children of six to seven. One school has on the time-table only an hour for the children of five to six and $1\frac{1}{4}$ hours for the children of six to seven, but in this school a good deal of extra work in these subjects is introduced in other lessons. Varied interpretations are given to such a term as 'occupations', and quite an amount of formal work is often done in times which appear to be given to informal activities. There is no doubt, however, that considerably more time is spent in reading, writing, and arithmetic in the control than in the experimental schools, and very little time is given to play in control schools after the children have passed the age of five. Systematic teaching in reading and arithmetic is given as soon as the children are five years old or even earlier.

THE TEACHERS

Care was taken in both types of school to use only classes which had been staffed throughout the children's infant school life by teachers who were recognized as competent, not only by the head teacher, but by their Local Authorities. While it was impossible to compare teachers exactly for their total ability as teachers and to avoid the possibility that head teachers who chose to work in one way may differ from those who prefer another, it was not the case that the class teachers had deliberately sought appointment in schools which followed one system or the other. They were appointed by their Local Authorities and in many cases changes of method in the school had taken place after their appointment. Two of the control schools subsequently changed their methods and the same teachers proved their ability to do good work on 'experimental' lines. It is unlikely therefore that the quality of the teachers could have been radically different in the different types of school.

CHAPTER II

HOW THE TESTS WERE CHOSEN

THE TEST OF INTELLIGENCE

BEFORE BEGINNING to test the children in order to find the results of their Infant School education, it was necessary to make sure that the groups of children tested in the two types of school were equal in as many respects as possible. It would be quite useless to compare older children with younger ones, or intelligent children with dull ones. It was determined, therefore, to form the two groups by pairing the children for age, sex, social background, and for intelligence. If, for example, there was in one experimental school a girl, aged six and a half, from a comfortable type of home, it was not only necessary to find a girl in the control school who conformed to these conditions, but also to make sure that the two children were approximately equal in intelligence as well. This meant that a test of intelligence had to be given.

It was impossible in the time available to test a large enough number of children by means of individual tests. Group tests were therefore examined. It was essential to find a test which did not require reading and writing. The Pintner-Cunningham Test was finally selected.[1]

This test is devised to measure the mental age of children between three years ten months and nine years seven months. It has been successfully correlated by its authors with the standard revision of the Binet Simon Tests in the case of 56 children, with the Otis group intelligence scale in the case of 75 children, and with teachers' rankings in the case of 81 children.[2] For the present research it possessed many advantages.

The small booklet attracted the children. It was found

[1] By Rudolph Pintner and Bess V. Cunningham, 1923, 1928. Published by the World Book Company, Yonkers-on-Hudson, U.S.A.

[2] See *The Prognostic Value of a Primary Group Test*, by Bess V. Cunningham. Published by Teachers' College, Columbia University. 1923.

that six-year-old children accepted the test eagerly and performed it with evident enjoyment, while five-year-old children did it quite willingly. The wording of the tests is clear and not too lengthy. Negative instructions are skilfully avoided which is extremely important in testing children at such a suggestible age. The word 'Don't' occurs only once.

The Test procedure was perfected by practice in using it with children not used as subjects in the final experiment. It was found that the children's scores nearly always approximated closely to their ages, except in the case of children who were judged by their teachers to be more or less intelligent than others of their age. The Head and class teachers were asked to place the children in what they judged to be order of intelligence, and it was found that their judgments generally agreed well with the test except in cases where the child was too young or too old for the class, this being, as Terman points out, a common source of teacher's errors in judging the intelligence of children.[1]

The Pintner-Cunningham test-matter consists of seven tests. The details of procedure and scoring are given in the manual of instructions accompanying the test.

During the first year's experimental work, the results of twenty-two children's tests were analysed in detail, and it was found that while some were too easy or too difficult for nearly all the children, others were divided fairly equally between success and failure. This was a satisfactory indication that the test was a suitable one for the children aged between five and six years to whom it was administered. It evidently allowed scope for children who were below or above their chronological ages to score at their own level. The test was later given to older children also, and it was found that even at seven years children did not score complete successes. When a test was needed for seven plus and eight-year-old children, however, a harder test was substituted.

The Pintner-Cunningham Test was repeated after a year's interval with twenty children aged six plus who had been tested first at five plus and it was found that in fifteen cases

[1] *Measurement of Intelligence.* Lewis M. Terman, 1922, pp. 24 and 25.

the difference between the second and first rating of the I.Q. was not more than 5. In three others it was not more than 8, and in only two was there a more serious difference, one child scoring 20 points and another 16 above his previous score.

When it was finally decided to use the Pintner-Cunningham Test it was administered first to children aged six plus who were to be used as subjects in the preliminary investigation, and also to children then aged five plus who were to be the subjects in the final investigation. The test procedure was strictly followed. In a few cases children who were obviously nervous or inattentive were re-tested later and credited with their second score.

The groups of children for the further tests were very carefully composed by pairing children for sex, age, and intelligence. The social background was not generally taken into further consideration than by the previous pairing of schools, but in a few cases, in schools where the social background was varied, care was taken to see that children were not paired with those who were very much poorer or more well-to-do than themselves.

In order to make the work as accurate as possible, very close pairing for age and intelligence was aimed at. For this reason the results of only about half the children originally tested in each of the tests were actually used. The final groups consisted of not less than twenty children from each school. Owing to the frequency with which children of Infant School age are absent from school through illness it was found best to test every child present and to form the groups according to those who were present for each test. On the whole the same children were used in each test, but sometimes, when children were absent, other children of equal intelligence and age were substituted.

The same person tested all the children, except in the reading and arithmetic tests (given after the outbreak of war) in Schools IB, IIIA, and IIA, where some of the children were tested by very reliable teachers in the reception areas. These teachers were very careful to follow the exact instructions given.

TESTS FOR THE RESULTS OF EDUCATIONAL METHODS

In selecting from a very extensive field of possibilities certain qualities and attainments for testing, the first question to consider was, 'What are the essential results of a good education for children up to seven or eight years of age?' This question involves the wider one, 'What should one reasonably expect of a "well educated" six, seven, or eight-year-old child?'

To look for skills and attainments or for qualities of character and personality which are not in keeping with the normal and healthy development of children at these ages would clearly be useless. It is important to consider what, in the opinion of experts in child psychology, is characteristic of six, seven, and eight-year-old children who have developed under favourable conditions. For example, a child of six and a half who has developed happily and normally in social adjustments to others will be capable of joining in another's game for a longer period than a five-year-old would do, and of sometimes setting aside his own interests to gratify another child's wishes, and will be beginning sometimes to see another child's point of view. To expect great sympathy for other children or sustained behaviour of a very unselfish kind would, however, be to look for what would be an unfavourable rather than a favourable sign at his stage of development. So, too, a very high standard of neatness and perfection of detail in writing and drawing may hint at faulty rather than at satisfactory developments, at seven years of age.

In choosing and in assessing the tests, therefore, the characteristics of happy and normal six, seven, and eight-year-olds respectively have been kept in mind.[1] It is, of course, recognized that children of a higher or lower intelligence will, particularly in intellectual matters, achieve very different results from children of average abilities. For this reason the children have been carefully paired for intelligence as well as for age, and tests have been chosen which offered scope for success at very different levels.

[1] Books which are of value in the general picture they present of normal development in children of different ages are referred to in Section II of the Bibliography.

Having reviewed the qualities and attainments which would be considered both by teachers and psychologists to be desirable in children by the end of their period in the Infant School, the next question was to consider which of these qualities it seemed possible to test, and which were most likely to throw light on any differences in the results of the different types of education given.

An important problem which has been seldom absent from my mind throughout this research is how one can be sure that the tests chosen really test the qualities they are intended to investigate. It is, of course, impossible to isolate qualities and abilities entirely from each other and many influences might be responsible for success or failure in the tests given. It was hoped, however, that by selecting tasks or situations which required a considerable degree of the quality or ability which it was desired to test, an indication at least might be given of its presence or absence, and that, by using four pairs of schools rather than one or two, differences which were due not so much to the type of education as a whole but rather to the particular teaching methods of different teachers might be recognized.

THREE TYPES OF TESTS

The tests given may be grouped into three classes, according to the further reasons for which they were chosen.

A

Some tests were selected to investigate qualities which it was possible might be less well-developed by education based upon play than by formal methods. In deciding upon these tests the opinions of teachers who believed strongly in formal education were taken into consideration. The most serious dangers which were contemplated were as follows:

1. The children might become incapable of concentration on a task in hand or of listening to directions given to them.
2. If they were allowed so much freedom to do as they wished, they might become selfish and inconsiderate of others

and incapable of settling down to a task which was not immediately attractive to them.

3. They might not acquire the power of persisting in the face of difficulty.

4. Their work might be untidy and careless.

5. Their standard in reading, writing, and arithmetic might be lower than that achieved by children who had received more formal training, and this lower standard in the Infant School might prove a handicap to the children in their later school life.

Such objections are worthy of serious investigation. By the time he is seven years old a normal child is capable of a considerable degree of concentration on a subject of interest to him. Mary Gutteridge found that children of five would concentrate for an average of forty minutes or longer on certain constructive activities and for twenty minutes or longer on seven other types of activity.[1] Dorothy Van Alstyne quotes sixteen and seventeen minutes for the average length of the longest time spent on materials by five-year-olds during separate observation periods of forty-five minutes.[2] There is no lack of evidence that the capacity for concentration develops as the child grows older, and therefore to lose this capacity would be a serious drawback and a form of education which resulted in its loss would have failed in an important direction. It was therefore determined to measure the length of time that the children in both types of school would concentrate upon a chosen activity.

The capacity to listen attentively and to retain what has been heard is again one which should increase as the child passes up the Infant School. The Binet Intelligence Tests for the repetition of syllables and digits give evidence of this; twelve syllables, for instance, are required at four, while sixteen are required at six years of age. The increasing complexity of the directions to be understood and followed in the tests is also evidence of the steadily increasing capacity of children

[1] *Concentration in Young Children.* Gutteridge, 1937, p. 7.
[2] *Play Behaviour and the Choice of Play Materials of Pre-school Children.* Van Alstyne, 1932, p. 36.

to understand and retain the meaning as well as the sound of the actual words spoken to them.

It would have been possible to test attention and memory in many different directions and for many types of experience, but the type of attention mentioned by the teachers undoubtedly meant the capacity to listen to and retain a teacher's words when used for oral instruction. It was decided to test this form of attention by presenting a descriptive passage orally to the children for illustration, and also by questioning them on a story read aloud. Since the anxiety felt by teachers was that the *capacity* to attend might be lost, it was decided to test the immediate recall of the passage read and not the long-distance memory of them. It was not inferred by any teacher with whom the question was discussed that education based on play was inimical to long-distance memory.

The question of investigating the possibility that the children might be less considerate of other children than those educated on more formal lines was the subject of much thought and some experiment which was afterwards abandoned. It was finally determined to rely upon six periods of observation of each child's behaviour under conditions of the greatest possible freedom.

Here again there is no lack of evidence that the children at six and seven should have progressed towards some forms of consideration for others. Very many researches on pre-school and also on older children have confirmed the fact that good social contacts increase with age. Jones and Burks quote no less than nineteen researches which give evidence of this kind.[1] Katherine Bridges records marked progress in this direction by the end of the pre-school period. She says, 'Between the ages of two and five years children in a nursery school progress from being socially indifferent infants, through the stages of self-assertiveness and interference with the liberties of others, to a stage in which they show consideration, sympathy, and kindness to others. They then delight in group play and co-operate with each other for mutual enjoyment.[2]

[1] *Personality Development in Childhood.* M. C. Jones and B. S. Burks, 1936, pp. 26–34.
[2] *Social and Emotional Development of the Pre-school Child.* Bridges, 1931, p. 85.

If such progress as this were lost rather than increased by the later work of the Infant School, it would indeed be an indictment of the methods used.

With regard to the capacities for effort, for persistence, and for willingness to undertake an uninteresting task if asked to do it for some sensible reason, such traits are undoubtedly signs of mental health and sound development, and in a moderate degree can be expected of children by the end of their period in the Infant School. It would not, however, be advisable to test these traits by imposing tasks which were so difficult that persistence would produce no result, or so purposeless that continued effort would seem to the child a sheer waste of time. Continued effort from young children under these circumstances would be evidence of over-anxiety in some form rather than of healthy vigorous development.

The test for willingness to undertake an uninteresting task (by requesting the children to do as much writing as possible with the idea of using the writing for making reading books) was also a test in persistence. So were many of the other tests, especially those in arithmetic in which close concentration on abstract numerical calculations was required. Some of the physical training exercises required persistence and effort of a rather different kind, although not for so long a period. The test of assembling geometric shapes to make pictures was not an easy one, and although it was designed to test ingenuity rather than persistence, it would be impossible for a child of six plus to do well in it without persistence and effort. It is true, however, that in this test the child himself would probably wish to make the effort, whilst in the writing test he is more likely to be making the effort for reasons outside his own immediate desires.

Had this trait been tested in children of seven plus and eight years as was originally intended, they would have been asked to do some mechanical practice with the motive of perfecting their own skill, because at that age such a motive will often appeal to children, but at the six-year-old level it was thought better to set before them the more direct purpose of producing a large amount of material which was to be used. At that age, as Charlotte Bühler[1] has pointed out, the child is capable of setting himself a task and working for a goal. She goes on further to state that: 'The child who undertakes a self-imposed task will accept one from another person,' a statement which does not suggest that schools in which children undertake self-imposed tasks, as they often do in their play, will produce children who fail to accept tasks from other people.

With regard to tidiness in work, although an extreme degree of neatness is not characteristic of the most intelligent and well-adjusted children at the age of six plus and seven, it is desirable that they should be able to carry out a simple exercise with their hands neatly and carefully if required, provided that it does not call for too great muscular co-ordination or straining of the eyes. The schools where the education is of the more formal type give in the handwork periods a good deal of instruction and exercises, with the idea of increasing the child's capacity to do neat work. It was decided, therefore, to give such an exercise in both types of school to see whether as a result of practice the children in these schools were actually superior in their ability to do neat and careful handwork. The results might, perhaps, suggest that the capacity to do neat and finished work matures as the child grows older and develops with general experience of handling materials, irrespective of the training given by special exercises at the Infant School stage.

B

Other tests were selected because they investigated qualities in which it was possible that children who were receiving an education based on play might excel those whose education was on formal lines. The most important claims made for this kind of education were:

1. The children were happier and more stable emotionally. There were therefore fewer problems of behaviour among them.

2. They developed greater initiative and ingenuity.

[1] *From Birth to Maturity.* Charlotte Bühler, 1935, p. 84.

3. They were more self-confident.

4. They were more imaginative or at least had a greater power of expressing their ideas.

5. They were more friendly and better developed socially.

6. Far from having less power of concentration, they had a greater capacity for becoming absorbed in a task than children who were accustomed to a more disjointed time-table.

7. Although they might at the age of seven be less skilled in reading, writing, and arithmetic, they had a greater interest in acquiring knowledge, which would cause them to do better work in these subjects by the time they reached the middle part of the Junior School, than children whose formal education had begun too early and absorbed too much time.

Some of the above characteristics could not be investigated within the limited time for this research. To investigate the very important questions of happiness, stability, and a good emotional adjustment would require a mass of detailed information about each individual child over a long space of time. Many workers in child guidance clinics and others interested in psychotherapy bear witness to the value of play in easing psychological conflicts and helping the child to achieve stability and happiness. Dr. Margaret Lowenfeld, in her book, *Play in Childhood*, quotes many instances of children whose emotional problems were to a great extent solved by rich opportunities for play. In her concluding pages she says, 'Without adequate opportunity for play, normal and satisfactory emotional development is not possible.'[1] My own work in play centres attended by the same children over a space of years has convinced me that many children who were previously considered difficult gradually ceased to be so when they found the kind of outlet in their play for which they were seeking, even though we were not qualified to use any special technique of play therapy.[2]

To obtain tangible evidence that the effect of the education given in the experimental schools of this research was to

---

[1] *Play in Childhood*. Margaret Lowenfeld, 1935, p. 324.
[2] *The Children's Play Centre*. D. E. M. Gardner, 1937, pp. 98–118.

produce stability and happiness and to help to solve emotional conflicts and problems would, however, have involved a very detailed investigation, not only into each child's behaviour before, throughout and after the Infant School period, but into home circumstances and the various out-of-school influences brought to bear on the child. It was hoped, however, that some evidence of the emotional stability of the children would be afforded by the six observations of each child's social behaviour which was undertaken primarily to investigate the degree of friendliness and good adjustment to others characterizing the children in the different types of school. Good social behaviour in young children implies good emotional adjustment. The children in the experimental schools certainly gave the impression to me and to other observers of being particularly happy, confident, and friendly, but these qualities are not easily tested.

It was decided to test ingenuity by means of a task involving the use of unfamiliar material to form pictures (see Test IV), and to test originality, richness of ideas, and the power to express them, both by this test and by one in free drawing and (at the age of eight) by written composition. Power of using words to express ideas was also to be tested by a series of oral language tests based chiefly upon exercises shown by their place in the scale of intelligence tests to be suitable for the comprehension of children of nearly seven. These were to be marked not, as in the intelligence tests, for comprehension only, but for the excellence with which the question is answered, the word defined, or the sentence formed. At the age of eight, language tests were to be given in written form.

It was decided to attempt to test the children's self-confidence by asking various assessors to rate the degree of confidence with which individual children tackled the problem of fitting difficult constructive toys together, their attitude towards failure, and also their attitude to the strange person giving this test. Later this test had to be discarded for lack of time, so this method of assessment, though showing promise, could not be carried on. A group test was decided upon of asking children to volunteer to perform a slightly alarming game instituted by a tester who had just met the group for the first time. This test, it was hoped, might give some evidence of the relative degree of certain kinds of self-confidence between children in the two groups. To obtain anything like conclusive evidence of every form of self-confidence would have been a long study. The manner in which the children tackled many of the tests would provide evidence of this kind, but not evidence which could be exactly measured. A second attempt to assess the attitude of the children to a strange adult was made by three independent observers who rated the attitude of the class as a whole to the teacher of physical training, a stranger to the class.

C

With regard to skill in school attainments, it was decided to test the children in reading, writing, and arithmetic at seven years of age, by which time a certain amount of skill in these subjects may reasonably be expected even of the slightly backward children, and one at which, in many districts, the children are promoted to the Junior Schools. These tests were to be given again at the age of eight, and in addition a test of written composition was to be given.

Drawing and language were to be tested at the ages of six plus and again at seven plus and eight. Physical training was to be tested once in the upper Infant School and again with the eight-year-olds.

The above subjects of the Infant School curriculum were selected partly because they represent important aspects of Infant School education: physical development, intellectual development, the acquisition of creative and expressive arts, and of the tools of later learning, and also because they are more easily tested than some other subjects of equal importance. It is difficult to devise adequate tests for such young children in subjects such as nature study, music, and literature, in which appreciation rather than skill or memorizing of facts is the criterion of successful teaching. The type of handwork done in the different kind of schools was so different as to make a common test difficult to find. The form of handwork which was most common to both, that is to say, modelling in plastic material, was the very one in which the practical difficulties of storing and preserving the products were greatest. Drawing was included in the curriculum of all the schools.

A further inquiry which might have been made was into the children's knowledge of their environment and of the lives of other people in their environment. The Sangren Information Tests[1] for young children were examined for this purpose, and would certainly have been tried but for the impossibility of finding time to add another test in which the children must be taken individually. It would have been desirable also to add to this test questions about the particular district in which the children lived.

A fourth and very important type of inquiry which might have been made would be to inquire into the children's physical condition by means of tracing the cause of absences from school and by examination of medical records. It is quite possible that the type of education given might have an influence on the child's health. It was originally intended to make such an inquiry, but the problems of the scattering of children by evacuation and the enforced absence from school of other children made it impossible to collect such data without throwing an unreasonable burden of correspondence upon Head Teachers.

PRELIMINARY WORK

A year was spent in experimenting with the tests by administering them to children, then aged six plus, in the same schools which were to be used for the final experiment. More time was given to tests which I had to devise for this research, than to tests which were already standardized and had a fixed procedure. This year's work led to many modifications of the procedure as originally planned. Methods of satisfactory scoring were also evolved. The detailed findings of this year's experimental work are given with the description of each test, but these may be briefly summarized here.

[1] By Paul V. Sangren. Published by the World Book Company, Yonkers-on-Hudson.

It was realized from the beginning that it would not be possible to obtain satisfactory results from this year's tests because so many changes of Head Teachers had taken place in the previous year. In only one of the experimental schools (School IIIA) had the children (then aged six plus) been educated on these lines continuously from five years old. In the other schools the children who would be six plus the following year and who were used for the final experiments had been under this régime for their whole school life, but the children aged six plus this year had experienced a gradually changing régime throughout the previous year.

The main purpose of this year's work was not to obtain results from the tests, but rather to perfect the method of giving them and scoring the results. For this reason it was not considered advisable to spend too much time repeating tests for children who were absent on the first occasion in order to bring the numbers up to twenty in each school. The children were, however, paired carefully for age and intelligence. The results, small as the numbers were, suggested certain tentative conclusions as a basis for work in the following year.

TENTATIVE CONCLUSIONS

The chief of these were:

1. The Pintner-Cunningham Intelligence Test would be satisfactory.

2. Children aged six plus in the experimental schools would probably be no worse than their controls in (i) concentration on an uninteresting task, (ii) listening and remembering what they had been told, and (iii) performing a task neatly and accurately.

3. They might prove better than their controls at (i) a task involving ingenuity, (ii) concentrating at an occupation of their own choice, (iii) expressing themselves by means of drawing, and (iv) performing a task needing self-confidence.

4. They would possibly be surpassed by their controls in the matter of handwriting.

SUMMARY OF GENERAL POINTS ABOUT TESTING CHILDREN OF THIS AGE CONFIRMED DURING THE FIRST YEAR

1. Children are very much influenced by the personality and skill of the tester and therefore it is essential that the same tester should do all the work in both types of school, and that she should be a person experienced in dealing successfully and happily with young children.

2. Any excitement, such as decorating for Christmas, a sudden snowstorm, or the imminence of 'bonfire night', can make it quite unprofitable to attempt any testing on such occasions. Whilst some children's behaviour is unaltered by such excitements, others are very much influenced by them.

3. Discomfort or unhappiness suffered by any child can completely invalidate a test, though it does not invariably do so. For instance, one boy who discovered that his new and valued coat had been soaked in water by another child, began his playtime by being very subdued, and when he finally began playing he followed others rather than accepted any leading role. This period was discounted as not likely to give a true picture of his social behaviour, and he was observed again on three other occasions. It was found that, though he was no longer depressed, the 'following' character of his play tended to persist, and that he did not appear to be a natural leader. However, there was a greater amount of play with others when he was not distressed.

4. Even slight fatigue can invalidate a test very easily. Postponement of playtime is inadvisable however convenient it may appear to be for the tester. It is most important that tests should be taken at the same time of day and after similar types of activity in the different schools.

5. A few months' difference in age can make a big difference to some of a six-year-old child's capacities. This was especially noticeable in the case of the test for colouring, cutting out, and mounting a picture.

6. Six-year-old children are much more easily influenced than are five-year-olds by the behaviour of other children.

Precautions to avoid copying are therefore more necessary with six-year-olds than with younger children. The five-year-olds, for instance, will generally ignore other children while doing the Pintner-Cunningham Test, but the six-year-olds and, still more, the seven-year-olds, will sometimes want to see what objects another child has marked.

7. Following established custom over little things has a tranquillizing effect on children and equality of conditions is better achieved by treating the children as they are accustomed to be treated than by attempting too rigidly to standardize every detail of procedure. Essential testing-points must, of course, be standardized, but there are many non-essential matters in the method of distributing material, giving permission to start work or share materials, or allowing these to be done without asking permission. It is best in such points to find out the procedure to which the children are accustomed and to follow it. Children of this age are easily disturbed by changes of procedure in what seem to us matters of detail. If it is necessary to depart from established custom, it is essential to explain this clearly to the children.

Charlotte Bühler's advice, although given for the testing of younger children, has been found very sound for the present investigation. She says, 'Under no circumstances should we attempt to obtain a purely mechanical similarity such as the physicist creates when he performs his experiments under the same physical conditions. We should, however, attempt to create a similarity which is adequate in our particular problem. . . . We do not try to obtain objective identity of experimental conditions but functional similarity—that is a similarity of stimulation for each individual.'[1]

8. Establishing a good relationship with individual children, and with the class as a whole, is essential to successful testing, but over-stimulation of the child's desire to please the tester should be carefully avoided. It is often necessary to treat individuals in the class in a different way to secure their best co-operation. One child will need encouragement of his efforts and the assurance that it does not matter if he makes

[1] *Testing Children's Development.* Bühler and Hetzer, 1934, p. 29.

a mistake, and other children need a quiet steadying word or become over-stimulated by much individual attention.

(It is, of course, very important that remarks made to encourage or calm an individual child shall not serve to help or hinder him in performing the actual test, but only to gain his best co-operation.)

9. A slight difference in the wording of a test can make it considerably easier or harder for the children, and it is necessary to observe strictly the form of wording and all pauses decided upon. The shorter and more simple an instruction is, the better will be the response. In many cases, details of instruction intended to be helpful have proved to be a hindrance, and the children's response found to be better when they were omitted. The pace of speaking, the tone and inflexion of the voice can also make a considerable difference, and it is wise to give instructions clearly and slowly without very much emphasis, since this procedure is more easily standardized than more emphasized speech. The slight formality suggested by this way of speaking has not been found to disturb the children. The tester speaks naturally and informally, except when giving the instruction for the tests.

10. Careful checking and arrangement of all necessary materials must be undertaken before the test begins and an adequate supply of occupations provided for children who finish the tests earlier than others. Attention to these matters secures a peaceful and happy atmosphere for the performance of the tests and sets the tester free to observe the children and secure accurate conditions of work for each child. If she is engaged in searching for materials she may fail to observe important points such as the children's helping each other or changing their work.

11. Unless an observer can be employed who is quite undisturbing and preferably a stranger to the children, and who can be relied upon to be quiet and to communicate only with the tester if necessary, it is better for the tester to be alone with the children. The presence of an assistant who fulfils the above conditions can, however, ease the tester's work, especially in testing groups over twenty in number.

CO-OPERATION WITH THE TEACHERS IN THE SCHOOLS

The administration of so many tests in any one school could easily become wearisome to the teachers, especially as tests must frequently be repeated for children who were absent on the first occasion of testing. It is therefore necessary to co-operate carefully with the school and avoid unnecessary disturbance and friction by:

1. Visiting the school only on occasions when the Head Teacher finds it convenient and avoiding days of medical inspections, etc., fitting in tests in accordance with the normal school programme as far as possible, and taking care to keep appointments punctually.

2. Whenever possible, providing the materials to be used, and if material must be borrowed from the school, notifying the school beforehand and assisting in getting out and putting away all materials borrowed.

3. As far as possible, showing the teachers results and tests in which they are obviously interested, and discussing these with them. This should be done after, not before, the test is finished, and no comparison between different schools should be made. Teachers, however, are often interested in the differences between the various children's performances and the relation of success to I.Q.

4. Avoiding making remarks which might be taken to imply adverse criticism of the children's responses, and showing appreciation of favourable responses.

5. Accepting good humouredly disturbances and interruptions, even though this may mean having to repeat a test at a later date. (However, after the first year, disturbances were nearly always prevented by explaining beforehand exactly what conditions were needed. It is best not to explain the actual purpose of the test. Some teachers knowing, for instance, that concentration was to be measured, might, with the intention of being helpful, urge the children beforehand to go on with their task for a long time.)

6. Reassuring teachers, if necessary, that it is understood that backwardness can be innate and not the fault of the

school, and explaining that work is needed for this research from children of all types of intelligence, not merely from the brightest children. Unless thus reassured, some teachers are unwilling to have the less intelligent children tested. It is often necessary to reassure teachers that, for instance, children aged six *should* fail in the harder Pintner-Cunningham Tests, as otherwise they are sometimes indignant at too hard a test being given and become apprehensive about other tests.

CHAPTER III

THE TESTS AND THEIR RESULTS
A. TESTS I TO V

(Approximate Age: 6½ Years)

TEST I A

Purpose. To compare the degree to which children in the experimental and control schools settle down to work at one subject or wish frequently to change their occupation.

Description of the Test. The children are provided with a choice of at least seven and not more than twelve occupations of a sort to which they are accustomed in school. Care is taken to see that the most popular activities are included, but nothing that is so novel or stimulating that it is likely to call out an unusually intense desire to continue for a very long time with the occupation.

In order to interest the children in the control schools, toys and apparatus which are usually available only for a free play period on Friday afternoons are put at their disposal, as well as handwork materials and school occupations. In the case of the experimental schools, the children are not invited to include such activities as free play in the hall, which is often allowed in their ordinary school programme, but which would probably be very much more attractive to them than anything which the children in the control schools would be in the habit of doing. In both cases, therefore, the toys and occupations are ones which the children are accustomed to using in their own classrooms. Reading, writing, or number games are always included, but these activities are supplemented by a choice of varied occupations and toys, selected because: (*a*) they are popular, and (*b*) they present opportunities for continuous work. An easy jig-saw puzzle, for example, would not be included, because on its completion the child would naturally put it away, whereas in the case of bricks, clay, or drawing he could continue for as long as his interest lasted.

The test is given after play in the afternoon. This is by no means the best time to obtain concentrated attention from young children. The purpose of the test is not to measure the absolute length of time for which the children can concentrate, but to compare the relative length of time as between the two groups. There is little doubt that earlier in the day many children would concentrate for a longer period.

The period allowed for this test is forty-five minutes if possible. In some schools unfortunately thirty minutes was the longest time available.

Points of technique discovered in the First Year. (Both for this test and for Test IB.) (*a*) The necessity for keeping the children in the classroom for the whole observation period. At first the test was given by asking children to leave the room as they finished their first occupation. This plan was found to be unsatisfactory. In some cases groups of children influenced each other. In one school a band of 'Cowboys and Indians' had a close organization and when the leader left the room the others followed suit. Others remained because they enjoyed the novelty of the test and the new tester, and therefore would not part with their occupations though they had ceased to concentrate on them.

(*b*) The necessity of seeing that the occupations were familiar ones. In one control school, toys were used which were seldom at the disposal of the children, and this caused them to become very excited and to interrupt their own occupation by asking other children when they could have their toys, or by trying to secure games and material which they had never had before. In another school, seven children obtained a maximum score on the occupation of cutting up coloured paper with scissors. It was found that this had not been allowed as an occupation by the school, and when the test was taken again without this occupation the children did not score so highly.

(*c*) The greatest problem was to provide equivalent conditions in the different schools. In School IB particularly the choice of materials available was not very attractive. However, it was found that painting was very popular, so it was permitted, even though the children had not had much experience with it. In this way it was hoped to balance the conditions more evenly between this school and School IA, where the children had many materials to interest them. To bring in a supply of new materials was likely to prejudice the children's concentration by providing a special incentive for changing from one to another. The reaction of young children in a poor district to new materials is nearly always to want to experiment with each in turn. With the plan indicated above it was secured that, in every school, material which was popular, but not too novel, was provided. This seemed to be the only possible way of making the conditions comparable.

(d) It was found that the longest spell of concentration was not inevitably given on the first occupation chosen. The type of occupation to which the longest spell of attention was devoted was therefore recorded for each child.

(e) It was found necessary to assure children, by a second reminder, that they might change their occupation when they wished to do so.

During this first year the test was given in two pairs of schools. In both cases the experimental school was superior.

Procedure for Tester. When the children come in from play, the tester shows them all the material. She speaks slowly and deliberately, naming each piece of apparatus as she shows it. She then says, 'Now you are going to choose one of these things to play with, and you can go on playing as long as you like, but when you are quite tired of it and you want to change, you are going to come and tell me. When you have got your things, sit down in your places and wait until I tell you to start.' The tester then organizes the children if necessary. For instance, in the formal schools particularly, it is often better to let the children come out a group at a time to choose the material. When they all have their chosen occupation the tester says, 'Now begin,' and notes the time.

After they have got well started she stops them for a moment and says, 'Now you can go on playing with these things as long as you like, but when you're quite tired of playing with them, come and tell me.'

(This reminder has been found necessary, since if it is not given the children often forget to tell the tester and it is then very difficult to score the test. The reminder has not been found to have a disturbing effect.)

If a child pauses for more than a moment or two, the tester says, 'Are you tired of doing it or would you like to go on?' Thus leaving the idea of going on before them, but not trying to influence them in any other way.

When a child says he wants to change, the time is noted, and also the occupation on which he has been engaged. He then chooses another occupation.

Remarks on children's reactions to the test. In three out of the four experimental schools, some children played together. In one school (IVA) this applied to as many as ten children, while five more shared paints very amicably. This did not affect the degree of concentration seriously—all were very much absorbed, chiefly in building. Number games were often shared in School IIIA, the children accepting arrivals and departures of other children calmly and carrying on the game with the inclusion of new-comers who arrived. Good social adjustment was very striking in this school. The majority of children chose occupations at which they worked alone, especially in the control schools.

In the experimental schools there were certain instances of children breaking off from an activity to help another child. If the interruption was only momentary and the child immediately returned to his own occupation the slight break was ignored in the scoring.

Examples. School IIA. One child lost a skittle ball. Several children helped him look for it. Kenneth stopped work to mix paint for Edward. On seeing me look at him, he said, 'I'm not changing, you know—just doing this for him.'

School IIIA. Dorothy spilt paint. Joyce said, 'Oh! you'd better get a floor cloth. I'll get it for you,' and she did so.

In the experimental schools the children were noticeably helpful about arranging and clearing up the materials and about reporting changes of activity. An observer used the terms, 'efficient, friendly, and sensible' in describing the children in School IIA during this test.

In the control schools the children were more passive, less capable in clearing up materials, and, particularly in School IB, very much more confused about reporting changes. They tended to ask for more help from the tester.

Examples. School IVB. Mary came to report having spilt the water. Tester replied, 'Well, wipe it up.' Mary did so, using her handkerchief instead of the floor cloth. Sheila (to tester), 'I say, what colour can you have smoke when you have no black?' (She is one of the most friendly children in the group.)

An observer reports: 'There was complete silence while the children were getting their things. Then many children began to say such things as, "I've got no water," "Please may I have some paper?", and yet all the materials were there and they had been told they might get them.'

In School IB several children would not draw without getting sanction from the teacher. 'Have I to draw a church?' 'Have I to put a bell in?' These questions were repeated even after several assurances that they might draw what they liked. There were also many children who said, 'May I begin?'

In the control schools the children seemed less sure of what they wanted to do at the beginning of the test. In the experimental schools the decision was usually taken quickly.

In School IA seven children chose reading books (of the picture-book type) and two number games, while in School IB these occupations were not chosen, though one child chose writing. Materials for constructive or expressive handwork accounted for most of the other choices. In School IVA reading was markedly more popular than in School IVB, ten children choosing it as against one child in School IVB. Over the schools as a whole twenty-eight children in the experimental and ten in the control schools gave their maximum period of attention to reading, writing, or number games. Too much stress should not be laid upon this difference, since the number games and reading books provided in the experimental schools are, on the whole, better chosen and more interesting to children than those provided in the control schools. However, the greater interest, especially in the books, suggests that the later beginning and less formal methods characteristic of the experimental schools may have a favourable effect on the child's attitude to reading. A study of the activities which were chosen, but did not gain the maximum length of the child's attention, again revealed a greater tendency to choose books in the experimental schools.

Method of Scoring. The maximum number of minutes spent by each child on any one occupation is scored, and also the number of times the child changes his occupation.

Method of Calculating the Significance of the Tests. The significance of all the tests is calculated by dividing the difference between the two sets of results by the average deviation of the difference. The average deviation is calculated by the formula:

$$\text{A.D. diff.} = \sqrt{\frac{\text{A.D.}_1{}^2 + \text{A.D.}_2{}^2}{N}}$$

A.D. diff. = average deviation of the difference.

A.D.$_1$ = average deviation of the scores in the experimental school.

A.D.$_2$ = average deviation of the scores in the control school.

N.   = number of subjects (which in this research is always the same and not less than twenty unless specifically stated in both schools in each pair).

The criterion of significance is taken to be:

$$\frac{\text{D.}}{\text{A.D. diff.}} > 3$$

Whenever $\dfrac{\text{D.}}{\text{A.D. diff.}}$ is 3 or above, the difference is regarded as significant. Some value may also be attached to results in which $\dfrac{\text{D.}}{\text{A.D. diff.}}$ is between 2 and 3.

This means that if the result is 3 or above 3, there can be no question of the difference in score between the two schools being due to accident. In these cases there is a real difference in result between the two schools, which cannot be attributed to the presence of a few exceptional children or any other 'accidental' cause. Some importance can also be attached to the results which work out between 2 and 3. They are unlikely to be due to any accidental cause. If the formula $\dfrac{\text{D.}}{\text{A.D. diff.}}$ however, comes to less than 2, no importance can be attached to the results.

SIGNIFICANCE OF RESULTS IN TEST I A

Schools	Maximum Length of Attention	Number of Changes of Occupation
IA & B	$\dfrac{\text{D.}}{\text{A.D. diff.}} = \dfrac{5 \cdot 3}{1 \cdot 06} = 5$	$\dfrac{\text{D.}}{\text{A.D. diff.}} = \dfrac{\cdot 70}{\cdot 21} = 3 \cdot 3$
IIA & B	$\dfrac{\text{D.}}{\text{A.D. diff.}} = \dfrac{5 \cdot 7}{2} = 2.8$	$\dfrac{\text{D}}{\text{A.D. diff.}} = \dfrac{\cdot 6}{\cdot 27} = 2 \cdot 2$
IIIA & B	$\dfrac{\text{D.}}{\text{A.D. diff.}} = \dfrac{1 \cdot 5}{2 \cdot 1} = 0 \cdot 7$	$\dfrac{\text{D.}}{\text{A.D. diff.}} =$ obviously less than 1 and therefore insignificant
IVA & B	$\dfrac{\text{D.}}{\text{A.D. diff.}} = \dfrac{10 \cdot 4}{3 \cdot 16} = 3 \cdot 3$	$\dfrac{\text{D.}}{\text{A.D. diff.}} = \dfrac{3}{\cdot 5} = 6$

N.B.—In this and all the other tests unless stated otherwise, the result is in favour of the experimental school. Cases in which the control schools are superior are recorded 'Against the experimental school'.

In two pairs of schools the results are significantly in favour of the experimental schools, in a third they tend to be so, although not quite reaching the criterion of 3. In the fourth pair, IIIA and B, the results are insignificant. It is possible that the test was given under conditions unfavourable to the experimental school as, owing to an interruption from the Head Teacher, the test could not be started until fifteen minutes later than usual, and thirty minutes only was available for the test. This meant that children who continued for the whole period had only the opportunity of scoring 30 points (four more of them scored a maximum in the experimental than in the control school). An epidemic of illness prevented the numbers from being up to twenty, and the intended repetition of the test was prevented by the outbreak of war. Only thirteen children in each of these two schools were scored.

It is possible that had the test been repeated under more favourable conditions the results might have proved more significant, as in the case of the other schools. It is quite clear that in no case was the length of concentration less, and that in two cases it was distinctly better in the experimental than in the control schools.

TEST IB

Purpose of the Test. To test the degree to which children in the experimental schools tend to do only what they find immediately interesting and the degree to which attention wanders unless the task is one which they would freely choose to do.

Description of the Test. Writing, especially copying from a book, is not a form of activity which usually appeals to six-year-old children. It requires considerable effort and close attention. It was therefore selected for this test. In order to guard against the possibility of the intelligent child considering such an occupation a waste of time and therefore abandoning it for a wise reason, it was decided to suggest that the writing should be used to make little books for children who needed something to read. No appeal was made to the children's pity for children without books. It was merely suggested that the books would be useful and that it would be desirable to write as much as possible.

An objection to the test is that in the experimental schools the six-year-old children have learnt writing for a short time only, while in the control schools they are more familiar with it and therefore require less effort. Seeing that this advantage was to the control, rather than to the experimental, schools, however, it was decided to try the test.

The test is given at 2 p.m. after the children have had half an hour in school, engaged in a quiet and restful occupation. As they finish writing they report to the tester and then take another occupation of an interesting nature, but not so stimulating as to distract the other children. The type of occupation resorted to by the teachers in the school for occupying children in odd moments is used—generally plasticine modelling or drawing with various materials.

Points of Technique discovered in the First Year. Points (*a*) and (*e*) as for Test IA apply to this test also.

Another point was the necessity of seeing that the alternative occupation provided for the children to do when they wanted to change should be pleasurable but not too stimulating. It was also found that a slight stimulation in the wording of the test was valuable. The idea of doing as much as possible was therefore emphasized more strongly.

The test was taken in three pairs of schools this year and the results did not show a significant difference.

Procedure for Tester. The tester provides each child with a pencil, a large sheet of plain paper, and a reading book containing stories, verse, or something suitable for copying. She says, 'Fold your papers like this (demonstrates), like a little book. Now *you* have all got some books to read, haven't you? Now I know some children who haven't, and they'd like some, so I thought you would copy out of your reading books in your very best writing into these little books and make them some. You'll do that, won't you?'

The tester then tells the children to start and after a little writing has been done (not more than three minutes at the most) she stops them and says, 'Now I want you to write as much as you can, but when you are *very* tired of it and really don't want to do any more, come and tell me, but you will go on as long as you can, won't you?'

If a child stops, but does not report, the tester goes to him and says, 'Do you want to stop now or will you do some more?' When a child asks to stop, the tester puts down the time and allows him to choose an alternative occupation.

Remarks on Children's Reactions to the Test. This test does not naturally call forth much enthusiasm but an attitude of friendly willingness to co-operate was noted in experimental schools IIA and IIIA. There was no actual opposition to the test in any school.

In one control school, IIIB, the children were evidently rather bored and restless, but seemed unable to believe that they would really be allowed to stop. Therefore, although their times appear long, the quality of the concentration was not in every case good. In the experimental school, IIA, some restlessness and not very good concentration was also noted. In the experimental schools the children were not afraid of stopping when they wanted to, and if they were in doubt they asked, 'Miss X, we're not forced to do *all* the books, are we?'

In experimental School IVA conditions outside the classroom were very disturbing, yet many children went on writing. In IVB there was no disturbance. In School IVA, too, conditions for writing were uncomfortable. There were insufficient tables and some children sat on small chairs, using large ones as tables. Their quality of concentration was, however, very good. They were not restless.

In two schools, one experimental (IIA) and one control (IVB), the children seemed to grasp the ostensible object of the test very well and take an interest in providing interesting books for the other children to read. In control school IB very little attempt was made to select interesting stories to copy, and some mere lists of words were copied: pig, wig, etc. In School IIIB the children were unable to get to work without asking such questions as, 'Have we to start at the first page?' 'Shall we start?', etc. Eight such questions were asked. In School IIIA they settled to work particularly quickly.

An interesting feature in this test was the degree to which children were influenced by other children's stopping work. It was not a very noticeable influence, except in the case of School IVB, where twelve children stopped work at the same time.

SIGNIFICANCE OF RESULTS IN TEST IB

Schools   Time of Concentration

$$\text{I}_{A\,\&\,B} \quad \frac{\text{D.}}{\text{A.D. diff.}} = \frac{4}{1.9} = 2\cdot1$$

$$\text{II}_{A\,\&\,B} \quad \frac{\text{D.}}{\text{A.D. diff.}} = \frac{1\cdot5}{2\cdot5} = 0\cdot6 \text{ (against the experimental school, but not significant)}$$

$$\text{III}_{A\,\&\,B} \quad \frac{\text{D.}}{\text{A.D. diff.}} = \frac{13\cdot5}{2\cdot4} = 5\cdot6$$

$$\text{IV}_{A\,\&\,B} \quad \frac{\text{D.}}{\text{A.D. diff.}} = \frac{12\cdot5}{1\cdot95} = 6\cdot4$$

Here again we find that there is no evidence of any experimental school being inferior to its control in the matter of concentrating on an uninteresting task. Again in two cases (Schools III and IV, this time), the experimental schools are very distinctly superior; in Schools I they tend to be superior and in Schools II the difference is less than one, which is quite insignificant.

Note.—In Schools III\ A and B the numbers were too small at first, and the test was repeated later with the result that the average age is 7 years 3 months, not 6 years 6 months, as in the other schools.

TESTS I I A AND I I B

Purpose of Test. To compare the ability of children in the experimental and control schools to listen to what they are told and to remember it.

To a certain extent, the Pintner-Cunningham Intelligence Test has tested attention, since success in it depends on the capacity to attend closely and to follow out instructions given. The fact that the children in each experimental school have scored at least as high as those in each control school,[1]

---

[1] Actually in the experimental schools fourteen children scored too high, in the Pintner-Cunningham Test, to be paired with children in the appropriate control school, while in the control schools only one child scored too high to be paired with one in the experimental school. The numbers gaining the lowest results were approximately equal.

indicates that they are not likely to be deficient in this direction. This cannot, however, be considered an exact measurement, so it was decided to try the two following exercises with groups of children whose intelligence, as given on the Pintner-Cunningham Test, were equal. The tests demand more sustained attention than the Pintner-Cunningham Test.

Description of Test. (*a*) A descriptive passage is read to the children and they are asked to draw the picture described. The passage was chosen from Dorothy Tudor Owen's *Child Vision*[1], and is a picture described by a child for other children to illustrate. It has been simplified a little for the use of such young children. It has been found that while no child has ever scored more than fifteen out of nineteen possible points, it is not so long and difficult that it wearied the children.

(*b*) The story given in the Merrill Terman revision of the Binet Intelligence Tests, *The wet fall*, is read to each child individually, and he is then asked the questions given in the test. As this test is included among those for eight-year-old children, it was thought to be sufficiently difficult to use with six-year-old children.

Time, 2 p.m. for (i); 3.30 for (ii).

Points of Technique discovered in the First Year. (*a*) The original passage tried was found to be unsuitable, chiefly because several children obtained all the eleven points which were capable of illustration, and also because there was a phrase, 'all the town', which lent itself to such varied possibilities for illustration that marking became difficult. The effect of experimenting with this test and its marking was therefore to abandon the original passage in favour of one of more exact and detailed description which lent itself more definitely to pictorial reproduction. In the passage finally selected nineteen points are actually mentioned which are capable of pictorial reproduction, and in marking it no other points were credited.

(*b*) It was necessary to provide chalks which showed up every small object clearly. The 'Maxam' crayons were eventually used, as they do not smudge.

[1] *The Child Vision.* D. Tudor Owen, 1920. Longmans Green & Co.

(*c*) It was necessary to have the test given by the same tester and in the same manner in both schools. On the one occasion where a different tester was used, she read the passage with more dramatic emphasis, and the results showed a striking superiority over those in any school tested by the usual tester. It was afterwards decided that the passage should be read slowly and clearly, but without particular emphasis on certain words or phrases.

(*d*) It was necessary to seat the children so that they could not easily see each other's work. In School Ib, particularly, there was a tendency to copy.

When the test was first marked an attempt was made to assess the drawings for boldness, vigour, originality of treatment and imaginative detail, and to add five marks if all these characteristics were strongly present, four if less strong, etc. It was then decided not to confuse the issue in this way, but to mark this test only for its particular purpose and to keep the question of artistic merit for a second test. It was decided, however, to ask an artist assessor to select the most interesting pictures to see if a difference was found between the number of children in the experimental and control schools who could combine accurate reproduction with artistic excellence. Nothing significant was found. No really interesting pictures were done, an indication, if one is needed, that the practice of asking young children to illustrate a descriptive passage heard, but not experienced, is not artistically productive.

In the two pairs of schools in which the finally selected passage was used the result was in favour of the experimental schools. Where the shorter passage was used no significant result was shown, and the work was found very easy by a good many children.

Procedure for Tester. The tester arranges the children so that copying is unlikely to occur, and gives out paper and 'Maxam' chalks. She makes sure that each child's box contains the colours which are essential for this test, i.e. blue, brown, green, and yellow. Other colours are also included.

She says, 'Now I am going to read you something, and when I have finished I want you to draw a picture about it

and put in as many things as you can remember. I am only
going to read it *once*.'

> 'There's a round open space in the middle of a big forest. And
> the trees are all green and you can just see the blue sky and a little
> bit of sun shining through the trees. And the grass is very green,
> and you can hear a stream, and there's a little brown rabbit under
> a big toadstool. And there's a bird.'

She reads slowly and clearly. Then she says, 'Now begin.'
If any copying is attempted she prevents it by saying, 'I want
you to do it out of your own head.' If necessary, she tactfully
puts a child in a different position. (Actually there was very
little attempt to copy, provided that the children were given
plenty of space.) No time-limit for the test.

As the children finish they bring their papers to the tester
and tell her what the objects represent, unless it is quite
obvious. She asks about anything that is not quite clear and
writes it on the drawing.

Remarks on Children's Reactions to the Test. The chief difference
was in the number of questions asked. There were far more
in the experimental schools.

IA. 'What was that thing you said first?' 'Did you say a
stream or a bridge?' 'Can you put in a man?'

IB. No questions.

IIA. 'Have we to colour the trees *all* green?' (A very
legitimate question in view of the description.)

IVA. 'Can't you put the *trunks* brown? They *are*.' 'I don't
know how to do a rabbit's face.' Several other questions.

IVB. Only one question all the time. 'What colour's toad-
stools?' But the children were pleased with the test and were
very careful and capable about giving out materials. They
shared crayons without any fuss.

IIIA. They were very patient and friendly over giving out
material.

IIIB. They were so confused that the tester had to do all
the giving out of material herself in the end. These children
were unwilling to share if a crayon was missing. They asked
the tester about this instead of asking another child, as the
children in IIIA did.

In the actual drawings there was a tendency in the experimental schools to remember the rabbit, toadstool, and bird whatever else was forgotten, and to forget the sky and grass more easily than did the children in the control schools. The tendency in the control schools was to remember sky and grass whatever else might be forgotten.

Scoring this Test. Points were given for attempts to represent objects described. The excellence of the drawing was not taken into consideration at all, nor was any notice taken of objects illustrated which were not in the original description. In some cases children introduced a good many ideas of their own in addition to illustrating the passage read.

One point was given to each of the following:

1. Any obvious attempt to leave an open space anywhere among trees.

2. Space in the *middle* of the forest.

3. Any attempt to show roundness of space. (*N.B.*—'Space' was sometimes interpreted by the children as a hole or indicated by a circle drawn on the ground. This interpretation was counted as correct. The test is not of comprehension, but of having listened and remembered the point read.)

4. Presence of two or more trees.

5. Trees (or one tree) *all* green. [Trunk allowed as brown, green, or any colour.] If some trees are green and others red or black the point is not given.

6. Blue sky. Sky is not awarded a point unless it is blue or blueish.

7. 'You can just see the blue sky.' Any attempt to hide the sky by trees. Actually no child did this, the sky, if represented, was always quite clear of the picture, or else drawn mechanically to the middle of the page before the drawing was continued.

8. Sun represented.

9. A 'little bit' of the sun.

10. Shining through the trees. If the sun is shown as a section rather than the whole circle two points are awarded instead of one because the child has remembered that it was 'a little bit of sun'. If, however, he has shown the sun from

behind the trees or drawn rays coming through the trees, three points are awarded. Some children drew one sun in the sky and a second piece of sun shining through the trees. This is given the full three points, the extra sun being ignored.

11. Presence of grass any colour.

12. Greenness of grass.

13. Presence of stream, though actually it is not strictly necessary to draw it. A great many children did draw it, however, so the point was counted as evidence of having heard it. If any child in reporting about his picture had mentioned the stream as not having been drawn, the point would have been scored, but this did not happen.

14. Presence of rabbit.

15. Brownness of rabbit.

16. 'Little' interpreted as being smaller than the surrounding trees, etc. Smaller or not very much bigger than the toadstool if present.

17. Presence of toadstool. The children sometimes interpreted the toadstool as an actual stool. This was scored as a pass. It only happened twice.

18. Rabbit *under* it.

19. Presence of bird.

If a child has copied another child the point copied is not scored.

SIGNIFICANCE OF RESULTS

Schools	Marks Gained
Ia & b	$\dfrac{\text{D.}}{\text{A.D. diff.}} = \dfrac{2 \cdot 1}{\cdot 63} = 3 \cdot 3$
IIa & b	$\dfrac{\text{D.}}{\text{A.D. diff.}} = \dfrac{1 \cdot 2}{\cdot 57} = 2 \cdot 1$
IIIa & b	$\dfrac{\text{D.}}{\text{A.D. diff.}} = \dfrac{2 \cdot 2}{\cdot 7} = 3 \cdot 1$
IVa & b	$\dfrac{\text{D}}{\text{A.D. diff.}} = \dfrac{1}{\cdot 76} = 1 \cdot 3$ (Against experimental school, not significant)

In two pairs of schools, I and III, the results are distinctly in favour of the experimental schools; in a third, Schools II, they tend towards significance in favour, and in the fourth pair they are against the experimental schools, but not by a significant amount. In three out of the four pairs of schools, therefore, the experimental methods have produced a greater capacity for listening and remembering, not less, as some teachers feared would be the case.

TEST IIB. FOR LISTENING AND REMEMBERING WHAT IS HEARD

During the first year a story was read to the children and they were afterwards asked to answer questions on it by means of drawing—since writing was too great a difficulty for such young children. It was found, however, too difficult to prevent children from the natural tendency to look at each others' drawings when in difficulties and while waiting for the next question. This difficulty scarcely arose when the whole passage was illustrated at once, and when the child brought his drawing to the tester immediately he finished, but when a single object only had to be drawn and the child could not remember the answer, the impulse to look was very strong. It was decided that the test must be given individually, in which case an oral test would be quicker and more easily assessed. The Merrill-Terman 'Memory for Story' test was used.

TEST IIB

Procedure for Tester. As in *Measuring Intelligence*, Terman and Merrill, page 233.

Say 'Here is a story about *The wet fall*. Listen carefully while I read it, because I shall ask you questions about it.'

Read:

Once there was a little girl named Betty. She lived on a farm with her brother Dick. One day their father gave them a Shetland pony. They had lots of fun with it. One day when Dick was riding on it, the pony became frightened and ran away. Poor Dick fell into a ditch. He was covered with mud from head to foot.

Ask the child the following questions and record his exact answers.

(*a*) What is the name of this story? (*b*) What was Betty's brother's name? (*c*) Where did they live? (*d*) Who gave the pony to them? (*e*) What did the pony do? (*f*) What happened?

The only differences between this test and that given in the book is the omission of the sentence, 'How Betty laughed when she saw him' (which makes the story rather long), and the omission of the direction to give the child a copy of the passage to follow while it is read.

Scoring. The test was scored as follows. The scoring is rather different from that given in the Terman and Merrill book.

Question. 1. 'What is the name of this story?' Two marks allowed, one for 'a wet', or any reference to wetness, and one for 'a fall'.

2. 'What was Betty's brother's name? 'Dick' or 'Dickie'. One mark.

3. 'Where did they live?' 'On a farm' or 'on their father's farm'. One mark.

4. 'Who gave the pony to them?' 'Their father' or 'Dick's father'. One mark.

5. 'What did the pony do?' Two marks allowed, one for 'became frightened', or any reference to fear, and one for 'ran away'.

6. 'What happened?' Five marks allowed. 'Dick fell' (1). 'Into water' (1). 'A ditch' (1).

(This means that 'Dick fell into a ditch' scores three marks. The term 'ditch', being unfamiliar to many children, it was thought advisable to allow a mark for remembering that he fell into something wet, even if the actual word were forgotten. 'He was covered with mud' (1). 'From head to foot' (1).)

As this test had to be given individually it was not possible to take it in all the schools. It was, however, taken in four schools chosen for their easy accessibility to the tester and her helpers. When the children were paired a great many fell out, so that the results of this test represent the achievement of twenty-eight pairs of children only. The children were selected purely at random, the test being given to every child present on the day of testing.

Results based on such small numbers cannot be very reliable, but they serve to indicate that the children in the experimental schools do not appear to be inferior in their power of listening and reproducing orally what they have heard. The comparatively equal result may be due to the test being largely one of general intelligence rather than of specific capacity.

TEST III

Purpose. To test the relative tendency in the experimental and control schools towards neatness and care in the use of materials for the performance of a set task in handwork.

In many schools the children are given frequent exercises in colouring, cutting out, and mounting pictures, or in similar exercises, with the idea of training them to do neat and careful work in general. In the experimental schools and others of the same type, such exercises are not given, but the children use handwork materials for their own purposes, and special neatness and care in the finish of their work is not asked for. This test requires the children to perform a task of the kind in which training is given in the more formal schools, but not in the experimental schools.

Description of Test. The children are asked to colour, cut out, and mount on stiff paper the objects in the picture shown on page 60. The picture is chosen because, although most of the curves shown are bold and not very difficult to fill in and cut out, there are others which are much more difficult and give scope for real skill. Care is taken to see that each child is given a pair of scissors with which he can cut, not too stiff, and with fairly sharp edges. The 'Maxam' chalks are given, and it is important that paste and brushes should be in good condition in all the schools.

Time. In the afternoon, after play, at 3 p.m.

In the first year it was found that the picture used was suitable. No child coloured and cut it out quite perfectly, showing that it was sufficiently difficult to make it a test of neatness and skill. Some children, however, did it very well, showing that it was not too difficult.

Points of Technique learnt. 1. The importance of standardizing the type of chalks, scissors, paste, and brushes. Inequality in these matters can be a seriously disturbing factor. Finally,

FIG. 1.

Reduced adaptation from the original illustration by Alec Buckels

'Maxam' crayons were used, fairly sharp scissors, small brushes, and paste of the consistency of 'stickphast'.

2. The importance of insisting that the colouring is completed before the paste is applied. The children themselves pointed out the necessity for this. If it is not done neat colouring becomes impossible.

The chief difficulty was in scoring the test. I scored the pictures several times to test my own reliability which I found at first to be only fairly good, but much better after devising a scale for marking. At first colouring and cutting out were assessed separately without reference to pasting.

A simple descriptive scale was first used, but gradually the more detailed and unified scale, given below, was evolved, as a result of experimenting with other assessors. It was decided to let three independent assessors use this scale in the final marking.

The test was given in three pairs of schools and the results in each case were very close indeed. Despite the fact that children in the control schools had frequent practice in such exercises while children in the experimental schools had little or none, the results seemed likely to prove equal. Since this is as important a result as any inequality, it was decided to adopt the test in its present form.

The test was given in a fourth pair of schools, but the results were invalidated by inequality of material. The control school had only pastel, which is very untidy for such work, while the experimental school had only pencil crayons. These, though less apt to smudge, made the work very slow and laborious, and certain children scribbled in order to cover the ground more quickly.

Procedure for the Tester. The tester gives out paste and materials before the children come in. She says to the children, 'Now I am going to give you a picture, and I want you to colour it. Try to make it very tidy and cut it out as well as you can and stick it on this piece of paper.'

When the pictures are distributed she says, 'Remember, *first* colour it, *then* cut it out, and then stick it on this piece of paper.' If the children forget the order or ask what to do next, the tester tells them. It is important to see that the children do not use paste before the colouring is done. No time-limit for the test.

Remarks on Children's Reactions to the Test. This test called forth a rather noticeably different response in the experimental schools from that in the control schools. This may have been partly due to the unfamiliar nature to the children in the experimental schools of the exercise. The teachers themselves were amused at the test, which confirmed the fact that they were not accustomed to giving such work. However, it seems unlikely that all the differences can be accounted for by unfamiliarity with the test.

A few comments are given by an observer in each school.

*Experimental I*A. Eager questions about the pictures. Jimmy was anxious to find out from his neighbour what colour a rabbit really was.

*Control I*b. No comments made by the children to the tester.

*Experimental II*a. The children were very noisy, but cheerful and friendly. Ian, 'If the head comes off, Miss X, they can easily stick it on again—we've got the paste.' Sheila, 'What shall we do the ducks if there's no white?' The children were very capable over the giving out and clearing up of materials.

*Control II*b. The children worked happily, accepted the task without much surprise or interest. Chatted to each other, but did not ask the tester anything.

*Experimental III*a. Much conversation. The children were cheery and friendly. David, thoughtfully, 'It's going to be hard to cut out.' . . . Later, looking at the swan, he said to himself, 'Now what colour should *that* be?' Elsie (also to herself), 'Now, shouldn't I leave my duck white?' Several children hummed while working.

*Control III*b. Not one comment from the children. They waited at each stage till reminded to go on.

*Experimental IV*a. The children settled down very quickly. Only one question from Mary. 'Have you to cut this out?' Friendly comments to tester. Barbara, 'There! I've done my ear wrong!' Tester, 'Never mind, I'll remember it wasn't as nice as you meant it to be.' A little later Walter said, 'Miss X, when you look at mine again, remember I tried to do this swan better, but I made a mistake.' Other remarks from time to time, e.g. 'The foot's slipped—the paste's too wet.' 'The swan's a bit off 'cos I thought it were dry and it weren't.' Very good at clearing up.

*Control IV*b. Very quiet. Coloured with great care. Tendency to wait for direction before passing on to the next step.

Method of Assessment. The work was examined by three independent assessors, all of whom were experienced teachers. The assessors were presented with a mixed packet of work from the experimental and control schools so that they were not aware which work came from which school. (This condition applied to all other tests by different assessors.) They were asked to arrange the work in five classes, being guided by the following description of characteristic features of each class.

Class 1. Good smooth colouring or shading. Cutting out following the line of the picture closely (deviation very slight and very seldom). Picture pasted flat on the paper.

Class 2. Quite good colouring. Cutting out fairly close to the lines, but over or under them fairly frequently by small amounts. Slightly crumpled by pasting.

Class 3. Colouring slightly untidy. Cutting takes out of picture or leaves on quite large pieces, but still keeps, on the whole, fairly parallel with the line of the picture. Some crumpling due to pasting allowed, but not very much.

Class 4. Untidy colouring. Large pieces cut out of picture or left on, but must be some clear attempts to follow the line of the picture. Crumpled pasting.

Class 5. Scribbled colouring or practically no colouring. Cutting out making no attempt to follow the lines of the picture. Very crumpled or not pasted down at all.

The assessors were not bound to make assessments exactly according to these descriptions, but were allowed to assess according to their impression, referring to the description in cases of perplexity, or as often as they wished

SIGNIFICANCE OF RESULTS IN TEST III

In these results the lower mark is better than the higher, since 1 denotes Class I and 5 Class V.

As the assessors agreed so closely, their marks were added together.

School   *Assessors' Total Marks*

$I_{A \& B}$ $\dfrac{D.}{A.D. \text{ diff.}} = \dfrac{0 \cdot 6}{1} = 0 \cdot 6$ Not significant

$II_{A \& B}$ $\dfrac{D.}{A.D. \text{ diff.}} = \dfrac{0 \cdot 9}{0 \cdot 96} = 0 \cdot 94$ Not significant

$III_{A \& B}$ $\dfrac{D.}{A.D. \text{ diff.}} = \dfrac{4}{\cdot 85} = 4 \cdot 7$

$IV_{A \& B}$ $\dfrac{D.}{A.D. \text{ diff.}} = \dfrac{1 \cdot 35}{0 \cdot 90} = 1 \cdot 5$ Not significant (against experimental schools)

6

In only one case are the results significant, and this is in favour of the experimental school. It is evident, therefore, that except in one pair of schools (III) there is no difference between the capacity of the children to do neat and accurate handwork of the type required by the test.

TEST IV

Purpose. To investigate the capacity of the children to perform a task requiring them to use ingenuity in assembling material which is not very suggestive into pictures imagined by *themselves*.

It was essential to choose an occupation of which the children had had no previous experience. It was found that while some of the children were accustomed to the use of coloured paper for pattern-making, none had had the experience of using an assortment of paper shapes for making pictures.

The test consists of providing each child with twenty-four coloured shapes, two each of: circles the size of 1d., ½d., and ¼d. respectively; crescents, isosceles triangles, right-angled triangles, squares, ovals, two pairs of rectangles of different sizes, and two irregular figures. The colours are always the same—grey for the square, orange for the oval, blue for the large circle, etc.

The children are asked to try to make a picture with the shapes provided. It has been found necessary to emphasize that a picture, not a pattern, is required. If children ask for other shapes than those provided they are told that the game is to see what they can make with the pieces provided, and new ones are not supplied. If they ask for scissors, the same reply is given. Tearing pieces is not forbidden.

This test is taken in the afternoon at about 3 p.m., when the children come in from play.

Points of Technique learnt in the First Year. At first it was thought that pieces of a suggestive shape should be given, for example, wheels, flower shapes, and shapes suggestive of parts of the body, etc. It was, however, decided to experiment,

FIG. 2

The above shapes have been reduced to one-third of the size of the originals given to the children. Their markings indicate various bright colours

first, by giving conventional geometrical shapes, and it was found that the children, especially in the experimental schools, made astonishingly interesting pictures with this very unpromising-looking material. It was therefore decided to keep the geometric shapes, since this provided a greater test of ingenuity than more suggestive material would do.

Other points realized were:

1. To warn the children not to make a pattern, but a picture. Before this point was emphasized many children made patterns, although a picture had been asked for. This year it was not scored against them since the point had not been clearly stressed.

2. To withhold scissors. In School IIIA the children asked for them and so transformed the test into another type of exercise. Tearing pieces was allowed, since this happened more rarely and only when the child felt the need to modify some special piece to meet a specific need. Scissors, however, could be used to make so many pieces out of the original shapes that it amounted to a use of almost unlimited raw material.

3. It was found that the very large shapes originally supplied (rectangles $6\frac{1}{2}$ inches by $1\frac{1}{2}$ inches, squares $2\frac{1}{2}$ inches by $2\frac{1}{2}$ inches, and smallest circle $1\frac{1}{2}$ inches diameter) were unnecessary. They took up so much room because they required double sheets of foolscap-sized paper for mounting that it was decided to test the use of smaller shapes on a single sheet of mounting paper foolscap size. The test was repeated with the same children who had used the larger size, and they were found to be just as successful with the smaller pieces.

4. The importance of refusing to supply extra shapes. In some schools children improved their work considerably by asking for fresh pieces, and other children then followed their example who probably would not have thought of it for themselves. In other schools no child asked for more pieces.

5. It was decided to standardize the colours, making all small circles green, etc., as it was thought that the colour of a shape was suggestive to a few children. On the whole,

however, they tended to ignore the suitability of colour if the shape suited their purposes and saw nothing unsuitable in, for instance, making the sun green or blue.

6. The necessity of asking and then writing on each child's paper what he has made. Sometimes when the explanation was given the result could be seen to be really ingenious, while without this, it was unintelligible to the tester.

7. The importance of giving each child a separate table and explaining that he must not exchange pieces with other children.

Method of Scoring. For a considerable time during the first year an attempt was made to score this test by counting the number of pieces used ingeniously. One point was counted for every shape placed to make something. Single shapes were not counted, even if named, unless they formed part of a picture or object. For example, if a moon was placed in the sky as part of the picture it was scored one, but shapes merely called 'moon' and placed anywhere at random were not scored, nor was 'ball', if merely appended to every circular piece, 'tent' to each triangle, etc., unless they formed part of a whole picture.

Torn pieces were counted if they were used, but extra points might be made in that way only up to ten, in order that the test might not be overweighted in favour of children who used this method. As tearing was not forbidden, its use was thought to show ingenuity if the needs of the picture demanded fresh pieces.

It was finally decided, however, to score the test by assessing the pictures according to their interest and value, taking into some account the number of shapes used, but not making this the sole criterion of success. Scoring by counting the shapes was open to the objections that pieces used in a rather obvious way scored as highly as pieces used really ingeniously, and also that unity in the picture received no more credit than many isolated objects put together by assembling two or three pieces. Experiments were undertaken by asking various assessors to place the pictures in five grades. In some cases the correlation between the method of counting and the method of assessment in grades was fairly close, as in the following scoring of children's results.

Child	Class	*Used Ingeniously Score in Counting Pieces*
A	I	22
B	I	30
C	II	20
D	II	21
E	III	14
F	III	17
G	III	15
H	III	13
I	III	20
J	III	14
K	IV	12
L	IV	8
M	V	5

The assessors were instructed to use certain simple criteria in deciding on a class. Later the fuller scale given below was evolved.

The test was found by experience to be fairly easy to assess, and the agreement between assessors was generally very close.

The results, which were taken in the first year from three pairs of schools, were all clearly in favour of the experimental schools. It has proved one of the most consistent of all the tests in this respect, both during the experimental and during the final tests, and by whichever method it has been scored.

Remarks on Children's Reactions to the Test. In Schools (i)A and IIA the children scarcely looked at each other's papers, but in (i)B and IIB they took a good many ideas from each other. In (i)B the objects were difficult to recognize and a great many children made decorated 'Easter eggs'. In the following year precautions were taken to diminish copying as much as possible, and if it were persisted in, marks were removed since it suggested a serious lack of ingenuity and resource.

In Schools (i)A and IIA extremely ingenious pictures were

made of a wide variety of subjects. In School IIB, rather few pieces were used, but more points were obtained by tearing, than in School IIA. In School IIB there was a tendency to place similar shapes together rather than to assemble them. In School IIIA every child used every piece he put on for some definite purpose. They used scissors. In School IIIB nine children out of twenty did patterns only, while in IIIA no child did so.

Procedure for the Tester. The tester provides each child with a table for himself, or at least sufficient space to make it unlikely that he will try to copy another child or mix up his shapes with those of another child. She provides also news-paper for the tables, paste and brushes, and a sheet of thick paper, foolscap size (for mounting the shapes). She says, 'I am going to give you these envelopes and there are some coloured shapes inside, and when you've got your envelope, I want you to shake out the shapes and look at them. Be careful to keep them on the desk (or your side of the desk).' She pauses while the children get the shapes out. Then she says, 'Make sure there aren't any more in your envelopes. They sometimes stick. You should have two of each shape.' She helps the children to check up. When she is sure that they have their shapes correctly, she says, 'I want you to make any picture you like with these shapes—*not* a pattern, a picture. Now begin.'

As they finish they bring their pictures to the tester, and she writes on the pictures exactly what they tell her that their pictures represent. If something is obviously intended, and yet the child does not name it, she says, 'And this?' She does not, however, press children to name every piece, as to do so would cause some children to invent names for objects which they did not intend when they put the pieces on.

Before taking the pictures away, the tester notices any pieces not securely pasted down and secures them firmly. It is also important for her to see that they are properly dry before gathering them together.

Notes on Children's Reactions to the Test. This test is very popular in all the schools.

In the experimental schools an observer noted some requests or pieces to be used for a definite purpose, e.g. 'I wanted to make a horse and cart, but I've nothing to make a horse with. I'll have to have that for its back, because there's nothing else.' They also asked questions about their pictures. 'Can I make two pictures? Could you have the sun *and* the moon? My sister told me so and I just wondered.'

In experimental school, IVA, nearly half the children assembled their shapes and studied the effect before beginning to paste. Many of them definitely rejected certain shapes from their pictures.

There were more requests for scissors from the experimental schools, but they accepted the refusal quite cheerfully. One advised another, 'You can tear, you know.'

On the whole, in the experimental schools the children settled down to work more quickly. In the control schools few comments or questions were noted.

In IVB, paper-cutting for picture-making was a weekly school occupation. This was the only school in which this exercise was taken at all regularly. The only difference noted in the results was a greater tendency to produce objects by folding and tearing the paper. This was an advantage rather than a disadvantage to the pictures in which it occurred. There were also more questions of the type of, 'Can you tear it pointed to make a horse? If you're doing a little girl, can you put eyes in?'

The results from this school, though better than those from the other control schools, were not as good as in School IVA (where picture-making with paper is not taught). It is just possible that familiarity with the material might cause the children in School IVB to have less zest over the task, but they did not show any sign of boredom when the test was given, so it is unlikely that their previous experience handicapped them in this way.

Some of the work from the experimental schools was strikingly ingenious and caused surprise to many people, including teachers who were accustomed to the work of six-year-old children.

Method of Scoring. This test has been scored by asking three assessors, working independently, to arrange the pictures in five classes. The assessors were all teachers with experience of children of this age. They had no special qualifications as artists. They were asked to assess the pictures for the ingenuity used in their composition. The following general suggestions were made to them after they had made their first rough classification on impression only.

Class 1. Should be an outstandingly good picture, should possess unity (since the test said, 'A picture,' not 'several pictures'), and should contain most of the pieces supplied. (It was considered that failure to use many of the shapes was not very ingenious. The sheets of paper for mounting were amply large enough to accommodate the shapes supplied. It was not, however, a condition of inclusion in Class 1 that *every* piece should be used.)

Class 2. *Either* two or more very ingeniously devised, but separate pictures, *or* one picture which is less strikingly ingenious than those placed in Class 1, but yet very good.

Class 3. *Either* two or more fairly ingenious pictures (even if there are other shapes placed at random) *or* a unified picture which is rather dull, with pieces put together in very obvious ways or with very few pieces used at all. (By 'obvious' is meant the assembling of only two or three pieces in very simple ways, for example, one triangle placed on a square and called a 'house' or 'church'.)

Class 4. *Either* one fairly ingenious object alone or among random pieces *or* two or more obvious or very dull ideas alone or among random pieces.

Class 5. *Either* pieces pasted on at random and named as single objects only, e.g. a circle labelled 'ball', a triangle labelled 'tent'; *or* pieces used for pattern only and not named; *or* only one very obvious idea among random pieces; *or* pictures almost entirely copied from another child's work. (The assessors were told when this had been the case.)

The assessors did not, on the whole, find the classification of the pictures very difficult, and their assessments agreed quite closely. As in all the tests marked by assessment, the differentiation of the middle class from Class 2 and Class 4 gave more trouble than deciding on Class 1 and Class 5. The assessors often wanted to revise their assessment of one pair of schools after dealing with other pairs. This was permitted. They were allowed to take their own time before coming to their final decision. They were not compelled to accept the suggestions made above, which were given only to suggest broad guiding lines and for help in difficult cases.

SIGNIFICANCE OF RESULTS

Since the assessors have agreed closely, the results are given by adding their assessments together.

Schools   *Assessors' Total Marks*

$$\text{I}_{\text{A \& B}} \quad \frac{\text{D.}}{\text{A.D. diff.}} = \frac{3}{\cdot 61} = 5$$

$$\text{II}_{\text{A \& B}} \quad \frac{\text{D.}}{\text{A.D. diff.}} = \frac{3}{\cdot 72} = 4 \cdot 2$$

$$\text{III}_{\text{A \& B}} \quad \frac{\text{D.}}{\text{A.D. diff.}} = \frac{3}{\cdot 6} = 5$$

$$\text{IV}_{\text{A \& B}} \quad \frac{\text{D.}}{\text{A.D. diff.}} = \frac{2 \cdot 9}{\cdot 77} = 3 \cdot 8$$

All the results are therefore significant and in favour of the experimental schools. There is no doubt that in this test for ingenuity all the experimental schools were distinctly superior to their controls.

TEST V

Purpose. To test (a) the artistic power of the children in the experimental and control schools, and (b) their capacity to express ideas through the medium of drawing.

The children were simply invited to draw a picture of anything they wished. At first it was thought that such an invitation would be too abrupt, especially in the control schools, and they were first asked to illustrate nursery rhymes.

It was found, however, that this tended to suggest to certain children, when free choice was afterwards offered them, that another nursery rhyme would be required, and experiment showed that the children were quite willing to begin at once on a subject of their own choice. A few children were inclined to ask the tester if they might draw a certain subject. In these cases the tester always replied in the affirmative. Large sheets of grey sugar paper were provided, twice the size of a sheet of foolscap paper. It was very difficult to find a medium which was suitable to the children in both types of school. The grey sugar paper was appreciated by both, but in most of the experimental schools paint was the medium most enjoyed, and in most of the control schools the children were not sufficiently accustomed to paint for a test in this medium to be a fair one. It was finally decided to use pastel, though this did not really satisfy the children in the experimental schools as much as paint would have done. The tendency of pastel to become smudged is a disadvantage. It is, however, a much more flexible medium for young children than pencil or crayon. In schools where the pastels were very poor, a set of Windsor & Newton's Ostwald shades was provided for the test. In the two IV schools a second test was given in paint to which the children in both schools were accustomed. There is no doubt that a good selection of tempera powder paint colours with large brushes gives many children of this age greater zest for their art work than pastel does. For this reason it would be unfair to compare work done in paint to that done in pastel. The test as it stands is perhaps slightly unfair to the experimental schools, but in any other form would have been distinctly unfair to the control schools, and the children in the experimental schools, though not so attracted by pastel as by paint, had had some experience in using it. During the first year's experimental work in one school, accustomed to both media, the test was given in both and the result of the painting was found to be superior in artistic merit to that of the pastel work. With some children the medium appeared to make little difference, but with others the paintings were undoubtedly superior to the pastel drawings.

During the first year it was also found necessary to ask the child to tell the tester about his drawing in order that she might give credit to his ideas. His description of his picture was written on the drawing.

Method of Assessment. This presented great difficulty. At first, after consultation with an artist who worked through 150 drawings with me, it was decided to adopt the following scale of marking.

Marked o. Drawings with nothing to recommend them.

Marked o+. Drawings with one feature of slight interest or value, but with no unity. No ideas or emotions expressed by the picture as a whole.

Marked i. Drawings in which the child was evidently trying to express ideas. An intelligent type of drawing, but not very clearly expressed.

Marked I. An intellectual type of picture in which the ideas were very well expressed.

Marked e. A picture in which the child has found an emotional outlet. There is evidence of enjoyment (for instance, in rhythmical scribble introduced into some of the pictures). There may be ideas expressed, but the accuracy of their reproduction is not the chief point of the picture.

Marked E. A very successful or striking picture of the 'emotional' type.

Marked a. Some artistic merit. The picture has unity, and a sense of balance between emotions and ideas. Good arrangement. Some sense of beauty expressed by the picture.

Marked A. A really artistic picture. Balanced, unified, and beautiful.

The results were assessed by the artist on this plan and tended to be in favour of the experimental schools. It was not easy to assess every drawing by the above classification. Many other assessors tried to do so and experienced difficulties. Some pictures fitted easily into one of the above classes and others caused much discussion and difference of opinion. It was finally decided to separate the factors of artistic merit and ability to express ideas and to ask assessors to put the pictures into five classes twice over for these separate qualities.

This meant that drawings previously marked 'o' and 'o+' were generally placed in Class V and IV respectively, and that pictures previously marked 'A' were almost certain of a place in Class I, both for artistic merit and for ideas. The two assessments, however, made the assignment of pictures to Classes II and III easier, and this had previously been the most difficult part of the work. Under the new system pictures previously marked 'E' and 'a' would probably be placed in Class II for artistic merit, while those marked 'e' and 'I' would probably be in Class III, and those marked 'i' in Class IV. Drawings which were beautifully arranged, but not very intelligible, could be placed higher for the 'A' than for the 'I' assessment. They had created one of the chief problems in assessment. On evidence of ideas, however, those marked 'I' would come into the top class and 'i' into the second class.

It was found much easier to come to a decision when there were fewer factors to consider. Experiments were conducted, and it was found that on the new system the raters' results correlated quite well, so it was decided to use this plan for the final tests.

The results were taken from five pairs of schools, three of which were marked in the first way and two on the plan which was finally adopted. In both cases the results showed the same tendency in favour of the experimental group. In fact, like Test IV, this test has proved consistently in favour of the experimental schools, however it was marked. The chief advantage in changing the method of scoring was that the new method saved the assessors much time and trouble.

In School IIB nine children out of the fifteen first tested drew conventional houses of very similar type, and their pictures contained little else. There was a tendency in this school to copy from each other the nursery rhyme drawings which were first given in this test. In School IIA the subjects were very varied. Many dealt with the daily lives of children; one, by a child whose home was unhappy, portrayed, all in black, a little boy shut into a large prison. Many drawings were of ships and aeroplanes, some of exploding bombs, one a particularly beautiful picture of the earth rushing up like a great fountain to meet a sky with clouds tossing in harmony with its motion. The drawings were much bolder and more decisive than in School IIB, and the colours used were more vivid.

Procedure for Tester. This test is given at 2.5 p.m. immediately after Test VII.

The tester asks the children to give out paper and pastels. As this test is given on the first day she takes this occasion to get on friendly terms with the children. When the material is distributed she says, 'Now I want you to draw me a picture about *anything* you like. You can do that for me, can't you? Now begin.'

If the children talk to her, she replies, but she is careful not to suggest anything with regard to the drawings. If a drawing is puzzling she says, 'Tell me about it,' and records the child's remarks, but she avoids other questioning, or in any way stimulating the children. They have as much time as they wish, and when they have finished they find another occupation.

Remarks on Children's Reactions to the Test. The chief difference noticeable was the very quiet response of children in the control schools compared with that of children in the experimental schools. In both cases the children settled to work easily and did not appear to experience difficulty in a choice of subject. Nor was a single question asked about how anything should be drawn. Details mentioned by an observer are as follows:

In Experimental Schools. IA. The children were very noisy, but happy, lively, and social.

IIA. The children were quietly absorbed.

IIIA. The children settled down at once very happily to draw. They lent pastels to each other with so little fuss that I often did not notice the lending until I saw the pastels being returned. They objected to the rather cramped conditions of their classroom, the desks being too small for their papers, and some children decided to sit on the floor. They did not ask if they might do this, but seemed to assume that naturally they could arrange themselves as sensibly as possible.

IVA. Three children were asked to give out paper. They discussed with each other a method of doing this, allocating different blocks of children to each. The class was rather noisy, but all the talk I heard was constructive and on the subject in hand. 'She means every one to have some.' 'Archie hasn't got any.' These comments were made to each other, not to the tester. Peggie, 'Miss X, the little girl next to me doesn't understand what we have to do, and I don't either.' Mary, noticing a late arrival, 'Oh, she's got no crayons, she can share with me.' All the children interchanged pastels when they needed a colour they had not got. This was done very willingly. They were also careful not to get in each other's way. They were absorbed and silent when work really started.

Painting test. Very unfavourable conditions. Thirty children in a very small room, using the floor. Insufficient paint jars. Yet they were orderly, friendly, and happy, and the results surpassed those in IVB.

Control Schools. IB. No comments at all from the children. They were very quiet.

IIIB. The children were very quiet. No comments or questions at all. They nearly all drew the sky first and then the ground before starting to draw any subject.

IVB. The children were rather quiet, but settled down at once without question to the task.

Method of Assessment. The drawings were placed, for artistic merit, in five classes by three independent assessors, who did not, of course, know from what schools the drawings came. One assessor was an art specialist in a training college, and the other two experienced teachers of young children with special qualifications in art.

It was not as easy as in Test IV to give the assessors any instructions, because the possibilities of variation were so much greater, owing to the greater flexibility of the material used. It was merely suggested that Class I should consist of outstandingly good pictures, the artistic value of which there could be no doubt, and that Class V should be those of no artistic value, while the other pictures were graded between.

There was, as might be expected, a greater divergence of opinion between the assessors than had been the case in Test IV, but still the agreement was fairly close, especially at the two ends of the scale.

The drawings were then assessed again for the richness of ideas expressed. It was found best to keep the two assessments entirely separate, and the assessors all agreed that the difficulties of assessment were considerably clarified when this was done. There were certain pictures which, while of no great artistic merit, were so interesting and full of ideas that the assessors hesitated to place them low, when they were trying to make one assessment only. One assessor said that in her opinion the children who drew these pictures were expressing in pictorial form ideas for which later they would probably use the medium of words, rather than of drawing. Another assessor described them as intellectual rather than emotional pictures.

There is a tendency for the Class I 'A' pictures to be very high in 'I' also, but it is not always the case.

Note on the Correlation between the Raters. This test was the one in which the raters differed most in their assessment of results. Therefore the correlation between the raters was calculated, and it was found that in the case of widest divergence, that is, between the first and second raters in Schools IA and IB for artistic merit, the correlation was ·65 and its probable error 0·05. Therefore the correlation divided by the probable error is 13, which is significant.

It was decided, therefore, that this test could be satisfactorily scored by adding the assessments of the different raters together as was done in all the other tests.

SIGNIFICANCE OF RESULTS

(a) For artistic merit.

Schools IA & B $\dfrac{\text{D.}}{\text{A.D. diff.}} = 4\cdot5$

„ IIA & B $\dfrac{\text{D.}}{\text{A.D. diff.}} = 3\cdot1$

Schools IIIA & B $\dfrac{\text{D.}}{\text{A.D. diff.}} = 4\cdot5$

" IVA & B $\dfrac{\text{D.}}{\text{A.D. diff.}} = 3\cdot5$ (Pastel)

" IVA & B $\dfrac{\text{D.}}{\text{A.D. diff.}} = 6\cdot1$ (Paint)

The results are therefore, in every case, in favour of the experimental schools, to a significant degree.

(b) For evidence of ideas.

Schools IA & B $\dfrac{\text{D.}}{\text{A.D. diff.}} = 3\cdot1$

" IIA & B $\dfrac{\text{D.}}{\text{A.D. diff.}} = 1\cdot9$ Not significant

" IIIA & B $\dfrac{\text{D.}}{\text{A.D. diff.}} = 6\cdot3$

" IVA & B $\dfrac{\text{D.}}{\text{A.D. diff.}} = 4\cdot2$ (Pastel)

" IVA & B $\dfrac{\text{D.}}{\text{A.D. diff.}} = 5$ (Paint)

The results are therefore, in three out of the four schools, in favour of the experimental schools, to a significant degree.

For artistic ability, therefore, it is clear that all the experimental schools are distinctly superior to their controls, while in the ability to express ideas they are superior in all cases but one, in which the superiority was not significant.

CHAPTER IV

THE TESTS AND THEIR RESULTS (*continued*)
B. TESTS VI TO XII

(Approximate Age: 6½ years)

TEST VI. LANGUAGE

Purpose of Test. To investigate the relative ability of the children in the experimental and control schools to express their ideas in words.

A series of language tests were given to children orally. The capacity of six-year-old children to write the answers would not be sufficiently great to make this a reliable means of assessing their capacity to use language. The administration of the test orally to each individual child was a slow process, and could not therefore be taken with very large numbers of children. Several testers shared the work, and although they followed precisely the same instructions there would inevitably be differences in the skill with which they administered the test, and got into *rapport* with the children. The testers were all students with some experience of dealing with young children. Their ability to gain the children's co-operation was shown by the fact that on later occasions many children asked for the test to be repeated. The children were taken at random from Schools IIIA, and IVA, and VA, and then paired with children of equal age, intelligence, and social background in Schools IIIB, IVB, and VB. The schools were chosen for their easy accessibility to the testers, but it happened that all these schools were in the more favoured districts socially. It might be expected, therefore, that the home would play a favourable part in the language ability of the children, and that they would be less dependent upon school in this respect than poorer children might be. Had the tests been given in poorer schools a greater difference might have been found.

One test which was originally included, but not here

Children outside a House
A. Experimental.   B. Control

A

B

Child in the Woods
A. Experimental.   B. Control

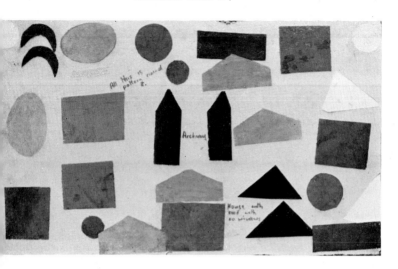

Ingenuity Test
Typical Control School Work

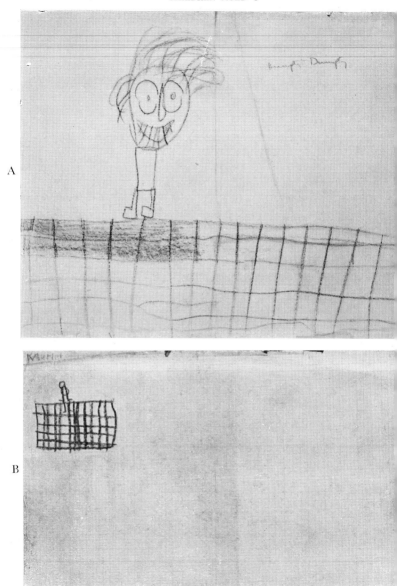

A

B

Drawing. 'Humpty Dumpty'
A. Experimental.   B. Control

Ingenuity Test
Typical Experimental School Work

man bouncing
two balls

clog

The sun

Two little girls and they are jumping
over some little toy stocks and
seeing who can throw
the ball highest.

Ingenuity Test
Typical Experimental School Work

Two suns and two moons

Two little ruins here

Two little houses here

Ingenuity Test
Examples of good Work in Experimental School

Ingenuity Test
Examples of good Work in Control School

Drawings showing People and Aeroplanes
A. Experimental.   B. Control

A

B

Landscapes
A. Experimental.   B. Control

A

B

Showing characteristic tendency of 'Control School' children to select
conventional subject and 'Experimental' to invent

Experimental: Bad boy escaping from Police.   B. Control: Father Christmas

Stories invented and illustrated by the child. There were very few examp
of these from the Control Schools

A. Experimental.   B. Control

A

B

Aeroplanes
A. Experimental.   B. Control

'Cowboys and Indians'
A. Experimental.   B. Control

A

B

Ships
A. Experimental.   B. Control

Ships and Aeroplanes.   A. Experimental.   B. Control

Note.—Contrast tended to be greater at 7 than at 6

reported in full, consisted of asking the children to describe a picture. Various methods of assessing the replies were used, and in every case the response of the two groups of children proved to be equal, as little as one mark of difference being found in the final results. It was therefore decided that the test might be too largely one of general intelligence to be useful as a language test, a conclusion which might have been expected from the fact that it is included in the Binet Tests, but which I hoped to avoid by more detailed methods of scoring than the procedure for the intelligence test allowed.

First Year. Owing to the time taken by giving the tests orally only twenty-four children were tested in the first year. The tests tried were naming pictures, questions on the pictures in the Pintner-Cunningham Test booklet, and the description of picture which was afterwards dropped. The children responded willingly, and there were no particular difficulties in giving the test. The method of assessing the answer was experimented with and the rating scale was evolved. The decision to use the vocabulary and sentence building tests was taken later.

Experiments in attempting to assess spontaneous language were made while children were playing with constructional toys and a toy village, but it was found that some children became absorbed in the constructive activity and did not therefore want to talk, though in the usual way they were fluent enough. Most of them did talk, however, at some time during the play, and had it not been for the time taken by this method further attempts to use it would have been made.

The use of the Kelvin Test booklet was not decided upon till the following year. It had the merit of being less absorbing to children, and of presenting many images in quick succession, some of which were likely to call forth comments, but the play material probably offered greater scope for richness of expression, especially if it could have been used on many occasions instead of merely on one. It was found, however, that the personality of the observer was an important factor in the test when toys were used. The children talked much more readily when with some observers than with others. Their play seemed to be an intimate matter and not so freely discussed as a picture-book. The best way of assessing their language capacity through the play would undoubtedly have been to take each child several times with the same observer, and it was reluctantly decided that to do this would be a further research in itself, and could not be combined with the present one.

Procedure. *Sub-test* (i). Naming objects from pictures. It was thought that the greater opportunities in the experimental schools for informal conversation between children themselves and between children and their teacher might possibly lead to the acquisition of a greater number of names for objects which are likely to be seen in picture-books or in daily life. The pictures on page 3 of the Pintner-Cunningham Test booklet were used as being a fairly representative collection. A good many of the objects illustrated are of animals which are not often seen by town children, so that to have acquired the correct names for these might be evidence of children having asked questions about picture-books or farmyard toys, rather than having overheard the names being used in everyday life outside school.

The objects illustrated are given below, and one mark is allowed for each one named correctly. Half marks are given for names indicated beside the correct name of the object.

1. Balloon or air balloon. 2. Tortoise. 3. Chicken. 4. Cow ($\frac{1}{2}$ for bull or ox). 5. Butterfly or moth. 6. Aeroplane ($\frac{1}{2}$ for aero). 7. Dog. 8. Kite. 9. Rabbit or hare ($\frac{1}{2}$ for 'bunny'). 10. Bird or the name of any bird which is anything like the correct shape ($\frac{1}{2}$ if very unlike, e.g. robin, wren, crow, etc.). 11. Pig. 12. Yacht ($1\frac{1}{2}$ marks), boat, ship, etc. (1 mark). 13. Wasp or bee ($\frac{1}{2}$ for fly). 14. Bat.

The maximum is therefore $14\frac{1}{2}$ marks. The results show a superiority of 17 marks for the experimental group, but this result is not quite large enough to be significant.

Test VI. *Sub-test* (ii) (*a*) *and* (ii) (*b*). This test consists of four questions based on the pictures in the Pintner-Cunningham Test booklet. The first two are aimed at investigating the capacity of the children to express clearly in words differences which they can observe quite easily in pictorial form. The little girls' faces and the houses on page 4 were chosen because they are the tests which the children find easiest. It is very rare to find a six-year-old child failing to select the 'prettiest' house or face, as required by the test, and this fact provides evidence that the differences must be observed.

(ii) (a). The child is shown the pictures of the three little girls' heads. The tester points to the second head, saying, 'Tell me how this little girl is different from this one' (pointing to the first).

The answers have been assessed as follows. Every answer given by the children whose results are entered below is shown under the mark given, unless the answer differs so slightly from the one given that there can be no doubt of its obtaining the same mark.

Marked o. No reply or one wide of the mark or one expressing no more than the question indicates.

Examples. 'Because it's not the same.' 'She isn't like them!' 'That's differenter than that.' 'They've nearly got the same faces.' 'She's nearly a bit different!'

Marked 1. Answers which do not express the idea of difference at all, which enumerate a list of features or point out one characteristic feature without comparison.

Examples. 'Her hair, eyes, or lips.' 'She has a thin neck.' 'She looks funny.' 'She has a nice face.' 'She hasn't got her hair cut.' 'Because she's turning this way.' 'She hasn't got a fringe.' 'They don't live together' (answer purely imaginary, but seems to justify a mark). 'That little girl is a bit laughing.' 'The mouth is all black.' 'Because she's smiling.'

Marked 2. Features pointed out as different, even if no description is given *or* description of several features, even if difference is not actually mentioned.

Examples. 'The hat's the same. The face is different, the dress is different.' 'She has nicer hair.' 'Her face is different —rounder.' ' 'Cos she's got longer hair.' 'This one has a nicer face.' 'This one is best.' '*Look* at that eye to that one.

Look at her! I don't like that one. Well, that one's better than her, isn't she?' 'The first one has scraggy hair. She has a point on her hat, a round neck on her dress.' 'She has different hair, different collar and eyes.' 'She's got a different neck. Her shoulders are different.' 'Her hair (first girl) is "wide".' 'They haven't got the same hair, they haven't got the same eyes. She's got curly hair and she's dressed differently.' 'By their faces, because this chin is this way (pointing to picture) and her chin's that way.' 'That one's got her mouth closed and that one's hair is straight.' 'That one has her hair down.' 'Their dresses are different.'

Marked 3. A comparison of the whole picture in general terms favourable to the prettier little girl, but without specifying 'prettier' *or* a specific comparison of one or two features, or very detailed description.

Examples. 'That one is going different in her eyes and lips. That one hasn't got her hair showing.' 'I like her best. Her face is nicest.' 'Her face is different—rounder.' ' 'Cos she's got longer hair.' 'Her hair is shorter. Hat is a bit different.' 'This one has a nicer face.' 'The first one has craggy hair. She has a point on her hat, and a round neck on her dress. She has a nasty mouth.'

Marked 4. A comparison of the whole pictures specifying that the one little girl is prettier *or* several specific comparisons of features.

Examples. 'She is a happier girl, nicer hat, face is not the same, the first girl's hair spreads out more. Her dress top is different.' 'The middle girl's the prettiest.'

(ii) (*b*). The child is shown the pictures of the houses, and the tester asks, 'How is this house (pointing to the third house) different from this house?' (pointing to the second house).

The answers have been assessed as follows:

No child failed to score a point.

Marked 1. One comment on a feature of one house, but without comparison, *or* a mere statement that one feature is 'not the same'.

Examples. 'The windows are wobbly.' 'Those windows are crooked.' 'The windows are straight.' 'It's got some funny patterns.' ' 'Cos the windows are all shuffled about.' 'Windows and the door are all mixed up.' 'Because there's no steps.' 'Because the windows are not the same.'

Marked 2. Two features described or one general comment on the house as a whole, still without mention of comparison.

Examples. 'The house isn't a proper house.' 'It has crooked windows. The door is on the side.' 'That one looks as if there's been an air raid.' 'The windows are crooked, the door's in the middle.' 'The other one is all over the place.' 'The windows and the door are took off and put in the corners in that one.'

Marked 3. One comparison on true grounds or three or more features described.

Examples. 'This one is best.' 'Because all the windows are crooked and these are not and the door isn't in the proper place.' 'The door's not in the same place.' 'It's got straight windows. The door's in the middle, there's a window over the door.' 'The second house is older, 'cos the door's in the side and the windows are not alike.' 'The third house has got straight windows while the second house has slanting windows.' 'This one has a crooked door and window and the door is at the side instead of in the middle.' 'It's a nice straight one. The windows are all crooked in the other.' 'This one isn't made (i.e. built) and that is.' 'That's got slanting windows and that's got straight ones.' 'Crooked windows, door in the wrong place—no step to it, only four windows.'

Marked 4. At least two clear comparisons of specific features or a good general statement of comparison.

Examples. 'This one's like a proper house, the other one has its windows all crooked.' 'These windows are straight, these aren't. This door is in the middle, this one is in the corner.' 'The second house is all crooked, the second house door is in the corner, the third house has the door in the middle.' 'There's no step in the second house, there is one in the third.' 'This has better windows than that. That door's at the side and that's in the middle.' 'It's got four windows and that's got five. That door's at the end and that's got it in the middle. None of them's got a knob on has they?'

Sub-tests II (c) and II (d). These questions are aimed at investigating the capacity of the children to provide a good word or simile describing the way in which the first two little girls on page 5 of the Pintner-Cunningham Test booklet are dancing. This test was one which interested the children, and on which they very frequently scored successes.

II (c). The child is shown the picture of the first little girl (page 5), and asked, 'How is this little girl dancing?'

The answers were assessed as follows:

Marked 0. Answers wide of the mark. No reply, 'I don't know.' Mere pointing out of objects. Mere demonstration, 'Like this,' or statements that she is dancing differently from the other child without specifying in what way.

Examples. 'I don't know how people should dance.' 'Her hands.' 'The girl is dancing different.' 'This one is dancing like this' (demonstrated). 'Because she can dance.' 'Because they're dancing.'

Marked 1. One comment on a non-essential point (i.e. points not descriptive of the act of dancing), or one difference not clearly specified between this little girl and the next.

Examples. 'Dancing like this because she's happy.' 'The first little girl has her arms out.' 'One arm high up.' 'With her feet out.' 'She moves her arms different.' 'Dancing on her feet.' 'She's dancing at a party.' 'That one's got a leg backwards.'

Marked 2. Two comments on true, but non-essential points. 'Tap dancing.'[1]

Examples. 'With her arms out. One of her legs out at the back.' 'With hands spread out—one hand higher than the other.' 'She is turning her toes out and jumping very high.' 'One leg down and one leg up.' 'She is tap dancing.' The others are all of the type, 'One leg on the floor and one off.'

Marked 3. Description of some characteristic of the actual dancing or three or more less essential points described or a good simile or an adverb which is not quite specific.

---

[1] 'Tap dancing' is awarded two marks because, although the movement depicted is not much like tap dancing, it is an attempt to describe the idea of dancing.

Examples. 'On her toes.' 'She's skipping with her arms out.' Like a fairy.' 'Nicely.' 'Toe-dancing.' 'She has got that foot at the back.' 'She is dancing like a bird.' 'One arm out there and one arm out there, one leg behind and one leg in front.' 'She's dancing with her foot forward and her other foot backward and her toes down.' 'She's lifting her feet up.' 'She's dancing lovely.'

Marked 4. One specific adverb or a very complete description.

Examples. 'She's dancing on her toes. Her arms are up in the air.' 'She's dancing prettily.' 'She looks light on her feet and her arms are spread out like a fairy or a flower.' 'She's dancing on her tip toes and her hands are out.'

Sub-test II (d). The child is shown the picture of the second little girl on page 5 and asked, 'How is this little girl dancing?'

The answers were assessed as follows:

Marked 0. 'I don't know.' No reply. Wrong answer, or one wide of the mark, demonstration only or mere pointing out of features in the picture.

Examples. 'On her tiptoes.' (Quite incorrect.) 'She's got her arms like this' (demonstrating). 'Because she can dance.' 'Her arms.' 'Dancing like that because the sun is shining.'

Marked 1. One comment not very important or appropriate.

Examples. 'She is skipping' (not appropriate). 'Oh, she's tap dancing too' (not appropriate). 'Arm not up, leg a bit crooked' (last point incorrect). 'She's putting her feet on the floor.' 'That one's got a leg forward.' 'She's got arms out too, like this.' 'She is dancing on the floor.' 'With one foot out.' 'She's dancing at a party, but dancing different because they don't want to dance the same way.'

Marked 2. A fairly good, but not very good description of the movement as a whole, or two comments on true, but not essential points.

Examples. 'She is walking.' 'With her arms out and feet out.' 'She isn't like the other. She isn't on her toes.' 'One leg down and one pointing up.' 'She isn't lifting up her leg as nicely.' 'Her feet stick out.' 'With both arms out like that —and one leg behind and one in front.'

Marked 3. Description of some characteristic of the actual movement as a whole.

Examples. 'Is she marching? I think she's marching.' (Quite possible from picture.) 'She's dancing on one leg.' 'On her heels.' 'She's making a noise as she is dancing. Her hands aren't as light as the other one's.' 'She's dancing on her feet, one arm is facing the ground.' 'This little girl is falling backwards.'

Marked 4. Very complete or vivid description of the movement.

Examples. 'She's not dancing proper. She's dancing with her arms out and with her legs stiff.' 'She's dancing like a wooden doll.'

SIGNIFICANCE OF RESULTS

$$\frac{\text{D.}}{\text{A.D. diff.}} = \frac{1 \cdot 9}{\cdot 46} = 4 \cdot 1$$

This result of this test is significant and in favour of the experimental group. It is evident that the children in the experimental schools could express their meaning more clearly and explicitly, when asked to answer the questions.

Test VI. Sub-test (iii). The Vocabulary Test, as given in the Terman-Merrill Intelligence Tests, is used, but the test is not scored merely for evidence of comprehension. It is used for assessing the children's power of expressing in words the meanings of the words given.

The wording used is that given in *Measuring Intelligence*, Terman and Merrill.

'I want to find out how many words you know. Listen, and when I say a word, you tell me what it means. What is an orange?'

Varying the form of the question and, urging the child if he hesitates, is carried out as indicated in the instructions for the test. The first eleven words are used. Fifteen words were originally tried, but so few children could even attempt the last four that they were omitted. Since the test did not produce a significant difference, the full scale of scoring each word is not given. Four only are selected as examples of the method of scoring.

Method of Scoring. (*a*) Orange.

Marked 0. No reply. 'I don't know.' 'It's an orange.'

Marked 1. Definition purely in terms of use ('What you eat.' 'You eat it.'), *or* one adjective ('round', etc.).

Marked 2. Some attempt at description, though only one point mentioned ('Juice comes out'), *or* definition in terms of use, and one quality pointed out ('To eat. It's juicy'), *or* two parts simply named, *or* 'a fruit', *or* one adjective and one part named ('It's round with all orange skin').

Marked 3. Three qualities described or two including 'fruit' ('Oranges are ripe. They are juicy, and good to eat.' 'It's red and it's round and it's got a thing on top where it grows').

Marked 4. Four qualities described, or three including 'fruit'. ('Round and it's orange coloured and inside it's very juicy and there's pips inside.')

Marked 5. A very good description, or five attributes described. ('It's orange colour. It has a star on top and pulp and pips inside. Sometimes there is a baby orange inside.')

(*e*) Puddle.

Marked 0. No reply.

Marked 1. Definition in terms of use. ('What you walk in.'), *or* one attribute ('It wets.' 'Round thing.' 'Muddy.' 'It splashes your stockings.'), *or* one poor synonym ('Pond.' 'Stream').

Marked 2. Clear indications that it consists of water without confusion with 'pond', etc. ('Water.' 'Rain.' 'The rain made it.' 'What rain makes when it stops raining.' 'Mud and water.')

Marked 3. A more detailed description or definition, but not a complete one. ('All water with soil that has gone soft.' 'A wet place on the ground.' 'It's all water, and when you step in it and start walking again, it makes footmarks.')

No one reached Class 4.

(*h*) Eyelash.

Marked 0. No reply. Merely pointing to eyelash or saying.

'One of these.' Wrong answer ('Eyebrow.' 'A whip') or wrong statement ('It's got hair on.')

Marked 1. Either a single statement of what it is ('It's all hairs'), *or* of where it is ('On your eye'), *or* a poor description, but some attempt at describing ('Sticking up and pointing downwards'), *or* poor definition in terms of use ('What you look through.' 'For eyes.')

Marked 2. Good definition of function ('Keeps muck from going into your eyes.' 'To keep the sun out of your eyes.') Statements which include *both* where and what eyelashes are ('Hairs on your eye'), *or* more exact statement of *either* what *or* where the lashes are ('What you wear on the skin over the eye.' 'It's all little hairs.')

Marked 3. Hair specified with a good description of where lashes are to be found ('Long hairs over your eyes.' 'A lot of little whiskers that hang over your eye.'), *or* good description ('An eye shade and a sun shade.' 'Sometimes they come off. They are short or long. You can blink with them.')

(*j*) Scorch.

Marked 0. No answer. Misunderstanding of the word ('Hop scotch.' 'Things you wash your clothes with.' 'Scorch kilt.' 'Cherries.')

Marked 1. Word applied in the correct sense though not defined ('You scorch your frock.' 'Fire scorches.'). One substituted word, not exactly correct ("Burnt") or one adjective ('All brown stuff.')

Marked 2. Description of how scorching takes place, e.g. reference to ironing something and scorching it—or leaving it too long before the fire, or pouring boiling water on yourself ('When things have been on too long. My father's shirt was.' 'Well if you put socks on the oven and leave them there—well, it scorches the socks.' 'When you're ironing and you scorch something.'), *or* description ('It makes a brown on a cloth.')

Marked 3. Good description ('When you put something over the fire and it goes brown.' 'A brown mark because it's hot.')

No one reached Class 4.

SIGNIFICANCE OF RESULTS

$$\frac{D.}{A.D. \text{ diff.}} = 1\cdot 9$$

The result, therefore, is not significant, although in ten out of the eleven words defined there is a slight superiority in favour of the experimental group. It would have been interesting to have repeated this test with children from a less favoured home background, since it is probable that the home played a large part in contributing to these children's vocabulary.

Test VI. Sub-test (iv). Purpose. To test the capacity of the children to form interesting and well constructed sentences, using three words given to them.

Description of Test. The test for sentence-building, given in the Terman and Merrill Scale for Intelligence Testing, is used, but it is assessed differently. It was chosen because, since it was standardized for children of seven years old it should be of the right degree of difficulty for children of six plus, but it is used here as a language test and not as an intelligence test, so that the replies are graded for value in power of expression, and also the capacity to form sentences is allowed some mark, even if all three words are not introduced.

Procedure. As in *Measuring Intelligence*, Terman and Merrill, page 157.

The tester says, 'I am going to tell you something about "dog . . . cat". "The dog runs after the cat." Now you make a sentence about

'(*a*) "Horse, bigger, dog."
'(*b*) "Boy, fell, leg."
'(*c*) "Child, flowers, garden." '

The word 'garden' was substituted for 'meadow' as being more familiar to town-dwelling children.

If the child hesitates he is encouraged, as indicated in the Terman-Merrill Test procedure.

Method of Assessment. Marked o. No reply. A mere phrase ('Another dog'), *or* one word incorrectly given ('The dogs bark.')

Marked 1. Two words introduced in note form, not as a complete sentence ('Horse bit dog'), *or* one word only introduced into the sentence ('He broke his leg.' 'Boy fell in ditch.' 'Flowers grow.')

Marked 2. Good sentence with only two words introduced ('The horse ran after the dog.' 'A horse is bigger than a cat.' 'The dog's an Alsatian, the horse is a horse.'), *or* all three words in note form (Horse bigger than dog.'), *or* all three words introduced in different and unrelated but good sentences ('A horse pulls a cart and there's a man on the cart. People grow big. And there's a dog which runs after a cat.')

Marked 3. Nearly perfect, but one word slightly incorrect ('A horse is a lot bigger than a big doggie.')

Marked 4. A sentence which is clear and grammatical and introduces all three words ('The horse is bigger than the dog.' 'The horse ran after the bigger little dog.' 'A horse saw a dog that was growing bigger.' 'A child is a lot bigger than a flower, but a garden can be a lot bigger than a child.' 'The child looked into the garden to see if the flowers were growing.')

SIGNIFICANCE OF RESULTS

$$\frac{D.}{A.D. \text{ diff.}} = 3 \cdot 1$$

This result shows that the children in the experimental schools were distinctly superior to those in the control schools in their ability to form good sentences using the words supplied.

Test VI. Sub-test (v). Purpose of Test. (A) To compare the degree to which children in the experimental and control schools will talk spontaneously to some one they do not know.

(B) To test the fluency and command of their language when used spontaneously.

The Kelvin[1] booklet for intelligence testing was presented

[1] *Kelvin Measurement of Ability in Infant Classes.* C. M. Fleming. Published by Robert Gibson & Sons, Ltd., 45 Queen Street, Glasgow.

to each child as a picture-book which he was invited to examine. This booklet is sufficiently like the Pintner-Cunningham Intelligence Test booklet to awaken memories of it and therefore presents the children with more opportunities for varied comments and conversation than an ordinary picture-book might do. The pictures are interesting to young children and portray a large number of widely differing objects. For the purpose of the test some pictures are drawn incorrectly or with missing parts, which facts often called forth comments from the children.

The children were tested by a student whom they had met only on the day of the test. They were, however, accustomed to the presence of students as observers, and each child had made a short contact with his particular student, by taking her out to show her the playground, early in the afternoon before the test was given. After this the students spent at least forty-five minutes as passive observers of the children's play before the test was given. The children were therefore accustomed to seeing the students using notebooks, both on this particular afternoon and on at least two afternoons previously. The students were instructed to behave as if they were engaged in writing entirely for their own purposes and not to appear to be glancing from the child to the book in a way that would cause the child to think his words were being recorded.

Procedure for Tester. At a moment when the child seems to have finished, or to be willing to break off from his former occupation, the tester goes up to the child and shows him the Kelvin booklet, saying, 'Here is a picture-book for you to look at. Come and sit by me and look at it. You may look at all the pictures if you like.' She then sits down beside the child while he looks at the book. She records verbatim if she can, but as unobtrusively as possible, any remarks which the child makes. She responds to these remarks in a friendly and interested manner, but refrains from asking questions or actively stimulating the child to further talk.

Notes on the Test. Sometimes a child spoke too rapidly and frequently for the student to keep pace with recording his speech, and she was able to give only a partial or partially descriptive account of what he said. The results, therefore, cannot be considered to be exact.

Another factor which militates against the exactness of this test is that the personality of one tester will be more encouraging to a child than that of another. The same students gave the test in the different schools, but even so, it is probable that in one school a less encouraging tester may have tested a child who was very confident, while in another she may have tested a child on whom she had an inhibiting effect. This test should really be given by the same tester to all the children, but there was not sufficient time for this to be done in the present investigation. Over a hundred children were tested individually.

Even with these limitations, however, the results are suggestive of greater fluency and command of language and greater confidence on the part of the children in the experimental schools, and therefore seem worth recording in the hope that at a future time the test may be carried out under more satisfactory conditions.

One difficulty which is almost impossible to surmount is that the child may not be in a 'mood' for looking at a book at the time when the test is given, and may therefore hurry through it while on another occasion the same child might be quite conversational and disposed to linger over the pictures. In two cases (both in experimental schools) the children showed an eagerness to dispose of the book quickly in order to return to their previous occupations. However, the test was given as far as possible at a time when the child seemed to have finished his previous occupation and to be ready for a change, and sudden interruptions were avoided.

A summary of the results when analysed for the fifty-two children paired for age, intelligence, and social background, is shown below. They are clearly in favour of the experimental group.

SUMMARY OF RESULTS

N.B.—In summarizing the results, no remark has been classified under more than one heading.

	Experi-mental	Control
Favourable		
1. Really good descriptive words or phrases	23	4
2. Clear statements of similarities and differences noticed between the different pictures	12	5
3. Keen enjoyment or humour expressed	6	2
4. Interest expressed in the purpose of the tests. (Some tests were actually performed verbally) . . .	4	1
5. Story related about one of the pictures	1	0
6. Fluency too great to be completely recorded. (These comments and descriptions were all of a high standard	5	0
7. Recorded sentences (or long phrases) of comments or questions about the pictures (other than those given in Nos. 1, 2, 4, and 5) . .	145	83
Not Favourable		
8. Many enumerations of single objects .	7	12[1]
9. A few enumerations of single objects .	1	1
10. No comments at all	5	5

TEST VII

Purpose. To compare the ability of the children to perform a series of exercises in physical training chosen with the purpose of testing their ability in certain specific directions. (For these see the separate Sub-tests.)

The exercises were chosen and conducted by a physical training specialist. The exercises were taken with twenty children, and the groups were paired as in the other tests. The apparatus used was taken to the schools so that there

---

[1] This includes the work of one child whose remarks were scarcely audible and of two who enumerated several objects incorrectly.

should be no variation in it. The same teacher took all the classes and used the same procedure and wording of commands each time. The children's response was either assessed by four independent assessors, or else, if actual success or failure could be noted, the number of successful or unsuccessful children was counted. The children wore coloured bands so that each assessor could count the failures or successes in one group only, and this economized time.

The lesson as a whole lasted about fifteen minutes. The school hall was generally used, but in the case of one pair of schools the playground was used.

Unfortunately, the test was not decided upon until the second year, so that preliminary work was not done with it. It was found that some exercises were very easy for all the children and did not produce any differences, since all the children tended to score successes. These exercises are summarized below and not reported in detail.

Exercises which did not yield significant results:

Exercise II. Ankle exercises, given to test the children's capacity to learn new movements.

Exercise III. An exercise in following the tester, given to test the children's quickness in moving into a formation.

Exercise IV. Given to test the muscular control of the children in changing from a noisy exercise (jumping) to a quiet one.

Exercise V. Given to test the quickness of the children to join up with a particular partner (boy with girl).

Exercises which either yielded significant results or which suggested that they might have done so if given with larger groups of children:

Exercise I. Purpose. To test (i) the alertness and energy of the children, and (ii) the speed with which they could adapt themselves to different movements, as they were suggested.

Procedure for Tester. Before the first exercise the tester gathered the children together and told them in a friendly way that she was going to see what they could do, and that they were to listen carefully as some of the exercises might be new to them. Then she said, 'Watch me and do as I do' (skipping). Then, 'Now pretend you are wooden soldiers' (running with stiff legs and arms). 'Now, rabbits' (hopping movement with 'tails up'). 'Now, hopping on one foot. Now kangaroos' (leaping). About two minutes was allowed for the whole exercise.

The response of the class as a whole was assessed for (a) alertness and energy, (b) adaptability. The following scale was used: Very Good (marked 1), Good (2), Fair (3), Lacking (4).

RESULT. TEST VII, SUB-TEST (i) A

	Assessors					Assessors			
School	A	B	C	D	Total	School	A	B	C	D	Total
Ia	1	1	1+	1+	5	Ib	1	2	2	2	7
IIa	1	1	1	1	4	IIb	1	1	1	2	5
IIIa	1	1	1	1+	4½	IIIb	3	3	3	2+	11½
IVa	1	1	1	2	5	IVb	2	2	2	2	8

SUB-TEST (i) B

Ia	1	1	1	1+	4½	Ib	2	2	2	2	8
IIa	1	1	1	1+	4½	IIb	2	2	2	1+	7½
IIIa	1	1	1	1+	4½	IIIb	2+	2+	2+	3	10½
IVa	1	1	1	1+	4½	IVb	2	2	2	2	8

SIGNIFICANCE OF RESULTS
SUB-TEST (i) A

Schools	Assessors' Totals	
Ia & b	$\dfrac{\text{D.}}{\text{A.D. diff.}} = 2\cdot3$	Not quite significant
IIa & b	$\dfrac{\text{D.}}{\text{A.D. diff.}} = 1\cdot5$	Not significant
IIIa & b	— —	Obviously significant
IVa & b	$\dfrac{\text{D.}}{\text{A.D. diff.}} = 4$	Significant

In two pairs of schools, therefore, the results are significant and in favour of the experimental group.

SUB-TEST (i) B

These results are all significant and in favour of the experimental schools.

These results indicate that in the matter of quick adaptibility to new instructions all the experimental schools excelled their controls, while with regard to alertness and energy they excelled them in two pairs of schools by a large amount.

Exercise VI. Purpose. To test the children's adaptability to rather complex instructions.

Procedure for Tester (who has in the previous exercise paired the children, each girl with a boy).

The tester says, 'Every *boy*, go and get a skittle, put it on one of these crosses,[1] and go and stand on *that* line opposite it. Every *girl*, go and get a ball and stand on *this* line opposite your partner.' The children who did not follow the directions quickly were counted. For this test no special method of calculating the significance has been used.

RESULTS OF SUB-TEST VI

Schools	Number who were Slow	Schools	Number who were Slow	
IA	2	IB	6	Obviously not significant
IIA	2	IIB	16	Obviously significant
IIIA	6	IIIB	20	Obviously significant
IVA	4	IVB	2	Obviously not significant against the experimental school

In two pairs of experimental schools the children were distinctly superior to their controls in following the rather complex instructions. In the other two pairs there was no appreciable difference.

Exercise VII. Purpose. To test co-operation with a partner

[1] Two lines and a row of crosses between were drawn on the floor previously.

in a way which requires more self-restraint than Exercise V does.

Procedure for the Tester. The tester says, 'Now the girls are going to knock down the skittles and the boys (you'll get your turn later), you are going to roll them back to your partner. Girls, see how many times you can knock the skittles down.' (Lets them play for two minutes.) Then she says, 'Stop! Now it's the boys' turn, and the girls are going to roll the balls back to their partners.' (Lets them play for two minutes.) The children put the apparatus away. The number of children who tried to knock down the skittles, instead of returning the balls to their partners, were counted.

RESULTS

Schools				Schools			
IA	.	.	. 15	IB	.	.	. 9
IIA	.	.	. 6	IIB	.	.	. 5
IIIA	.	.	. 5	IIIB	.	.	. 3
IVA	.	.	. 10	IVB	.	.	. 7

In Schools IA and IB only was the difference significant. It is against the experimental school. The results are not very significant, and it was a difficult test to mark, but there is a slight indication that the children in the control schools were better at obeying the instructions given, and that if given with larger numbers of children the test might have proved in favour of the control schools. One drawback to this test was that it is obviously a better game if each side takes it in turn to aim at the skittle rather than if they follow the instructions as given. It is also sometimes difficult to be sure whether a child who returns the ball to his partner and knocks down the skittle in doing so has done it intentionally or unintentionally. For these reasons it was decided to remove this test and substitute for it free play with the skittles and balls so that it could be seen which children co-operated and which kept the apparatus for their own individual use.

This was actually done in Schools IVA and IVB, with the

striking result that in School IVA nineteen of the twenty children played together with the skittles, while in School IVB only two did so, the others using the skittles and balls as individual playthings. However, unfamiliarity with such apparatus may have accounted for that.

Unfortunately the outbreak of war and the evacuation of the children made it impossible to carry out this test in the other schools.

Exercise VIII. Purpose. A. To test the speed and self-control with which the children could choose and start playing with varied apparatus. *B.* To find out how many children chose to play together.

For purpose *B* the test proved a failure, as the apparatus provided was not used co-operatively except by three children in all the eight schools. The skittles, perhaps because they had just been used in the previous exercise, were not usually chosen, while skipping ropes and hoops are playthings which are more often used individually than co-operatively by young children. It is possible that the children were reacting from the forced co-operation of the previous exercise, and that if a longer period had been allowed some of them would have joined with others later on. The free play with skittles and balls, as suggested above, would probably have been a better test.

For purpose *A*, however, the test was useful. There was much opportunity for crowding and confusion in getting the apparatus from the piles placed in corners of the room, and there was also the possibility of quarrelling when popular apparatus was used up.

Procedure for Tester. The tester says, 'In the corners of the room you will find ropes, balls, skittles, and hoops. Get any bit of apparatus you like and play with it. If you want to play with a partner you may.'

The test was assessed on the following scale for quickness and absence of 'fuss' in getting to work with the apparatus. Very quick (1), Fairly quick (2), Fairly quick, but confused (3), Slow (4), Disorderly (5).

RESULTS. SUB-TEST VIII

Schools	Assessors				Total	Schools	Assessors				Total
	A	B	C	D			A	B	C	D	
Iᴀ	1	1	1	1	4	Iʙ	3	3	3	5	14
IIᴀ	1	1	1	1	4	IIʙ	2	2	2	2	8
IIIᴀ	1	1	1	1+	4½	IIIʙ	2	2	2	2	8
IVᴀ	1	1	2	2	6	IVʙ	3	3	3	3	12

The results in every case are significant and in favour of the experimental schools. The children in these schools were quicker and more co-operative about getting out this apparatus.

An attempt was made to test the ability of the children to relax, but in many cases the idea of relaxation exercises was new to them and they did not easily grasp what was required. It was also difficult to judge of relaxation by merely looking at the children. It was decided, therefore, to test the children individually, at a later date, when time could be taken to convey the idea of relaxation to each child so that the tester could be sure that failure to relax really meant inability to relax. The dispersal of the children by evacuation made this investigation impossible to carry out.

During the first attempt the assessors were agreed that in Schools IIIʙ and IV.ʙ, the whole class appeared rather tense, and that in the corresponding experimental schools this was not the case. On the other hand, in Iᴀ and Iʙ the number of children who appeared unable to relax were nine and five, and in IIᴀ and IIʙ six and two against the experimental schools.

General Assessment of the Relation of the Class to the Tester. The assessors were asked to award one of the following marks to the class as a whole:

1 Very friendly and responsive.
2 Friendly and responsive.
3 Fairly friendly and responsive.
4 Passive obedience only.
5 Not responsive.
6 Refusal to co-operate.

RESULTS

Assessors					Assessors				
School	A	B	C	D	Total	School	A	B	C	D	Total
Ia	1	1	1	2	5	Ib	2	2	2	2	8
IIa	1	1	1	1	4	IIb[1]	1	2	1	2	6½
IIIa	1	1	1	1	4	IIIb[2]	4	4	3	3	14
IVa	1	1	1	1	4	IVb	2	2	2	2	8

Significance of Results. In Schools IIa and IIb, where the difference is the smallest

$$\frac{\text{D.}}{\text{A.D. diff.}} = 3\cdot4,\text{ which is significant.}$$

It was evident, therefore, that in all cases the children in the experimental schools were distinctly more friendly and responsive in their attitude to the stranger who gave the tests.

TEST VIII

Purpose. To find the number of children who have sufficient confidence to volunteer to perform a test which places them in an unknown situation.

This test seems to require two kinds of confidence. (*A*) Trust in an adult who is a stranger to the children. (*B*) Self-confidence on the part of the child, shown either by his expectation of success in an unknown situation, or by his attitude of fearlessness towards possible failure.

The test is a Montessori game, but one which was unfamiliar to any of the children tested.

It is given the first time the tester meets the class, and it is deliberately worded in a way which is not very reassuring. If the test were given after the tester were known and trusted by the children, it would be less useful.

[1] The assessors agreed that while this class was friendly and energetic their control was not always very good, for instance, the children kicked the skittles over instead of following the tester's directions.

[2] This class began by an attitude of passive obedience only, but progressed to being fairly responsive and friendly towards the end of the lesson.

Points of Technique discovered in the First Year. At first the test was given by asking the children to volunteer to come out in front of the class to say nursery rhymes. This was done before the test in drawing was taken, and it was found to be disadvantageous to the drawing test. It was also decided that a test which involved playing a strange game and one which, moreover, required the child to be blindfold would be a better test of self-confidence than a request to perform a common school exercise such as reciting. The number of children who volunteered to say rhymes was greater in the experimental than in the control schools. The test in its final form was taken this year with one pair of schools only, and the results were as follows:

Experimental	*Control*
18 out of 23 children volunteered to play the game.	4 out of 15 volunteered.

Procedure for the Tester. The tester says 'Good afternoon' in a friendly way, but does not enter into conversation with the children. She asks the class teacher to leave the room. She then produces a large scarf and says, 'I'm going to play a game and some one must have this tied round their eyes. Who will?'

She notes the number of children who volunteer; she chooses one who does so and asks him to stand on a chair. She then blindfolds him and hands to him one by one four objects, such as a brick, scissors, a cloth, and a bottle. The child guesses what he is holding.

The tester then asks for another volunteer, and again notes the number of children who are willing to do it. This second situation is different from the first in that the children now know what will be required of them, but there is a possibility that the idea of having unknown objects placed in the hands might prove alarming to children unless they have confidence in the tester.

Owing to the necessity for this test to be given the first time the tester met the class, it was impossible to give it to groups paired as in all the other tests. It was taken with all the children who were present on the first day, and although it would have been possible to form groups by pairing these children, to have done this would have been to reduce the numbers to very small ones. To have tested at a later date the children who had been absent on the first occasion would have been hardly comparable since by that time the tester was on friendly terms with the other children, and this would have been evident to the children who had been absent.

This test, therefore, is not claimed to have been taken with groups of children who were precisely equal in age and intelligence. The number of volunteers out of the number of children present are shown. The groups were not specially selected, and are not likely to have been very different from the point of view of age and intelligence. They were approximately equal in social background. This test, however, can only be regarded as suggestive in its results, and needs extending to larger numbers of children more closely paired.

Remarks on Children's Reactions to the Test. Experimental Schools.

IA. The children were interested and amused. Much laughter.

IIA. The class seemed interested. Pleasure was shown when the blindfolded child guessed correctly.

IIIA. The children showed amusement and appeared friendly to the tester.

IVA. There was pleased and friendly laughter at the guesser's success. When the second child had finished guessing they said spontaneously, 'Now you have to pick some one,' thus adapting the game to the rules of other games familiar to them.

In the control schools the children were much quieter. In School IVB the children smiled when the guesser succeeded, but in the other schools this response was not so evident. In School IIIB the children were very serious, and very few smiled at the tester.

The results are expressed as a fraction, the numerator showing the number of volunteers, the denominator the number of children present.

RESULTS

	Experimental				Control		
School		1st	2nd	School		1st	2nd
Iᴀ	. .	$\frac{11}{27}$	$\frac{8}{27}$	Iʙ	. .	$\frac{3}{22}$	$\frac{7}{22}$
IIᴀ	. .	$\frac{16}{34}$	$\frac{15}{34}$	IIʙ	. .	$\frac{5}{21}$	$\frac{5}{21}$
IIIᴀ	. .	$\frac{7}{14}$	$\frac{7}{14}$	IIIʙ	. .	$\frac{5}{27}$	$\frac{5}{27}$
IVᴀ	. .	$\frac{10}{21}$	$\frac{10}{21}$	IVʙ	. .	$\frac{4}{27}$	$\frac{3}{27}$

N.B.—The same number in the second column as in the first indicates an extra volunteer, because the original child never volunteered a second time. The difference between the number of volunteers the first and the second times they were asked for is not significant.

The main difference lies in the number of original volunteers, nearly half the children volunteering in all the experimental schools, and in the control schools approximately one-seventh, one-fourth, one-fifth, and one-seventh respectively.

This test suggests that if carried out with larger numbers a very significant difference might be found in the number of children who would volunteer to perform a task requiring self-confidence.

TEST IX

Purpose of Test. To compare the social interactions among the children in the experimental schools with those in the control schools.

In the first year an attempt was made to assess, on a five-point scale, the child's attitude to another child who was allowed to share a toy village after he had played with it alone for about ten minutes.

This procedure was not found to be very satisfactory, since it made a considerable difference to some children which particular child happened to be chosen to play with him. It was decided that to observe on six occasions the child's spontaneous social behaviour when at play with his companions in his usual school surroundings was more likely to give a true picture of his stage of social development than the attempt to observe it in a situation created for a test. This plan meant that the children had a choice of companions and met many children in one period while under observation, whereas in a specially planned situation they would be in contact only with a few. The playground was first selected as providing three valuable conditions for successful observation of social behaviour, freedom from restraint, absence of toys and materials which might distract the children's attention from each other, and equality of conditions between the experimental and control schools.

It was considered, however, that it would be valuable to supplement this observation by observing also a free occupation period in the classrooms so that the social reactions between children when they had materials and toys to play with could be observed. The chief difficulty attending this piece of observation was the inequality of conditions within the schools. Everything possible was done to obviate this inequality; toys and materials of a fairly similar kind were provided, and in the case of School IVb, where very little equipment was available, toys were supplied for this experiment; but even so, the traditional standard of quiet in the classrooms of this school doubtless had its effect on the children's social behaviour. In some control schools the children were accustomed to a period of play with toys once a week.

It was decided to observe each child (both in the playground and in the classroom) on three separate occasions with at least three weeks' interval between one observation and another so that exceptional causes of particularly social or unsocial behaviour should not have too much influence. If a child was known to be particularly excited or upset for an unusual reason he was not used for the experiment. The length of the observation periods was fifteen minutes in the playground and thirty minutes in the classroom. As each child had to be observed individually three times, very large numbers of children could not be used. They were drawn from the same schools as for the language tests; that is to say, from the schools with the more favoured social background. The same observers who gave the language tests kept the records of social behaviour.

Procedure for Observers. The following instructions were given:

'Observe the child in the playground and again in the classroom for the whole time allowed. Note every occasion when he approaches, has any contact with, or deliberately holds himself away from another child. If possible, note the length of time he plays with others. Note *exactly* what he does and if possible also what he says to other children, every helpful act, every quarrel, etc., in as much detail as you can give. If you have time, record also what the child plays with, either when with other children or when alone. Try not to let the child be aware that you are watching him.'

Note.—There were unfortunately certain gaps in the observations recorded. The observers, not being specially trained for such work, did not always realize the significance of detail, and occasionally, though not often, recorded general statements, such as, 'Played together with the shop,' when more information was needed. They had been instructed to observe as unobtrusively as possible, and it was often difficult to catch a child's actual words or follow all his rapid movements in the playground, and yet to keep him unaware that he was being watched. The observation of children under five is easier in this respect than of children aged six and a half. Some of them are very quick to notice an observer, and then become reserved or anxious to attract attention.

Analysis of Records. The social contacts here recorded from 174 observations in both classroom and playground cannot be claimed as an exhaustive record of every social response, but most of each child's social reactions have been recorded.

TEST IX (i)

Playground Observation of 58 Children

(Made during three fifteen-minute periods of undirected play.)

	Experimental Total Number of Occasions	Control Total Number of Occasions
A. Friendly behaviour towards other children.		
1. Joined together for a definite game .	14	2
2. Looked for and joined special friend .	13	3
3. Talked for quite a long time to another child about the flowers or any interesting objects near at hand .	10	2
4. Attached himself to a group of other children	28	9
5. Asked to join others, but did not join without asking. (This showed a desire for companionship, but rather suggested lack of self-confidence.) .	0	7
6. Games mutually agreed upon of a mock aggressive character, friendly fighting, etc. (It was noticeable that some children in the Experimental Schools responded by playful, but not by real, fighting to interference or damage done to their buildings, etc.)	29	8
7. Organized games well. The child appeared to be popular and was accepted as a leader . . .	15	7
8. Invited or was very willing to accept another child into his game . .	12	5
9. Accepted cheerfully accidents caused by another child to himself or his property, or teasing or (once) adverse criticism	13	7
10. Showed sympathy or protected a child who was hurt, unfairly treated, or at a disadvantage	15	6

	Experimental Total Number of Occasions	Control Total Number of Occasions
11. Acquiesced in another child's suggestion, showed willingness to take turns or to accept an uninteresting role for another child's pleasure . .	19	9

No significant differences shown.

	Experimental	Control
(a) Skipped or ran in company with another child	42	39
(b) Helped others or lent property . .	10	8
(c) Shared toys (perhaps appears a larger difference, but the 12 points are taken from 2 children only) . .	12	5
(d) Talked or listened to a group of children	8	9
(e) Occasionally friendly gestures . .	2	0
(f) Acted as peacemaker in a quarrel .	1	5
Total .	75	66

	Experimental Total Number of Occasions	Control Total Number of Occasions
B. Friendly attitude towards adults.		
1. Talked to adults in a friendly, natural way (without self-consciousness) .	28	7
2. Asked for help from adults (numbers not significant)	—	3

C. Responses called forth by a social situation which cannot be classified as social or anti-social. Numbers not significant.

1. Insisted on fair play for himself . .	3	0
2. Played with younger child rather than one of his own age . . .	0	3

	Experimental Total Number of Occasions	Control Total Number of Occasions
3. Cried on being hurt, but quickly recovered	3	0
4. Protested without aggression . .	0	4
5. Refused a challenge to fight . .	2	1

D. Unfriendly behaviour towards other children.

1. Refused other children's friendly gestures or invitations to join a game .	0	9
2. Deliberately took or tried to take other child's toy or spoilt his game . .	0	12
3. Pushed or hit another child without apparent provocation . . .	1	8
4. Refused to welcome other child into his game or let him have a turn in a game	0	8
5. Unnecessarily aggressive in defending own rights	0	7

No significant differences shown.

	Experimental	Control
(a) Ignored other child's distress . .	1	1
(b) Laughed at other's mishap . .	0	1

E. Solitary Attitude.

1. Stood about doing nothing for most of playtime—at a loss for occupation .	0	9

No significant difference shown.

(a) Chose to play alone for part of the time	15	15
(b) Watched game with interest, but made no attempt to join in . . .	6	3
(c) Tore about by himself 'letting off steam'	2	3
(d) Very few social contacts at all during the entire period	2	2

F. Negative attitude to adults.

Very little was recorded and nothing of significance. Points noted were:

	Experimental	Control
1. Self-consciousness in speaking to adults	I	2
2. Rather officious in helping the teacher	0	I
3. Showed evident satisfaction in doing a forbidden thing	0	I

TEST IX (ii)

Classroom Observation of 58 Children.

(Made during three thirty-minute periods of undirected activities in the classroom).

	Experimental Total Number of Occasions	Control Total Number of Occasions
A. Friendly behaviour towards other children.		
1. Contributed willingly to the work of the group and accepted responsibility in the group, e.g. by taking less pleasant role to further the purposes of the group . . .	19	2
2. Shared toys and apparatus willingly, and took turns happily . . .	40	14
3. Invited other child to join game or use toys	15	I
4. Helped other children or advised them constructively	46	22
5. Showed or commented on own occupation to another child . . .	39	14
6. Questioned, praised, commented on, or looked with friendly interest at another child's occupation . .	75	21
7. Acquiesced co-operatively in other child's wishes and suggestions .	15	I
8. Discussed or chatted over work with another child	14	6
9. Played with special friend (the same child as in the playground) . .	14	2

9

		Experimental Total Number of Occasions	Control Total Number of Occasions
No very significant differences shown.			
(a)	Shared jokes with other child . .	8	2
(b)	Independent of group, yet friendly to it	4	0
(c)	Cheerful acceptance of chance teasing or accidents	2	1
(d)	Interceded to get fair play for another	2	0
(e)	Comforted other child . . .	2	0
(f)	Occasional friendly gestures (e.g. smile, pat on back in passing) . .	3	0
(g)	'Aggressive', but mutually agreed upon games	6	1
(h)	Showed power of both leading and following	6	0
(i)	Always led and offered better ideas .	7	2
(j)	Made social response though absorbed in occupation	5	0
		45	6

Though individually these miscellaneous social responses are not different by a significant amount, there is a considerably greater total of them in the case of the experimental group.

B. Friendly attitude towards adults.

1.	Asked adult for reasonable amount of help and information . . .	12	2
2.	Talked to adults in a friendly way .	25	12
3.	Showed work to the teacher . .	10	3

Numbers not significant

Reminded others of the teacher's orders .	2	0

C. Responses called forth by a social situation which cannot be classified as either social or anti-social. (Numbers not significant.)

	Experimental	Control
1. Justifiable and not unfriendly resistance to aggression or interference .	7	0

	Experimental	Control
2. Protested without acting aggressively .	4	3
3. Double reaction, first aggressive, then friendly	0	2
4. Sought to win the group's attention by dramatic method	1	1
5. Did not stand up for his own rights effectively	0	1
6. Tried and failed to persuade others to play with him	0	1

D. Unfriendly behaviour towards other children.

There are very few instances recorded and they are almost all of different kinds.

	Experimental	Control
1. Aggressive response to chance pushes, blows, etc.	1	0
2. Refused to accept other child into game	5	0
3. Took best toy for himself . . .	0	1
4. Direct refusal to request for help .	1	1
5. Ignored other child's distress . .	0	1
6. Defended his own rights aggressively .	0	1
7. Attained his ends by force . .	0	1
8. Pushed past other children . .	0	1
9. Gave help unwillingly . . .	0	1
10. Ignored friendly gestures and remarks from others	0	4
11. Refused to exchange toy . . .	0	1
12. Ignored other child's need of help .	0	1
13. Laughed (unkindly) at other's mishap	0	1

	Experimental Total Number of Occasions	Control Total Number of Occasions
E. Solitary attitude.		
1. Very little or no social contacts . .	4	43

	Experimental Total Number of Occasions	Control Total Number of Occasions

F. Negative attitude to adults.

Very little recorded and nothing of significance. Points noted were:

(a)	Aware rather self-consciously of adult observers	1	3
(b)	Rather fussy and over-anxious to make contact	0	1
(c)	Rather formal and shy . . .	0	1
(d)	Minimum response possible to adult's advances	0	4
(e)	Disobedience (deliberate) of teacher's orders	0	1
		—	—
		1	10
		—	—

Summary of Results

TEST IX. A. PLAYGROUND

Average Age: 6 yrs. 6 months   Average Age: 6 yrs. 7 months
Average I.Q.: 111·6   Average I.Q.: 111·2

Experimental		*Control*	
Total of good social responses . .	=274	Total of good social responses . .	=138
Total of anti-social responses . .	= 3	Total of anti-social responses . .	= 50

TEST IX. B. CLASSROOM

Experimental		*Control*	
Total of good social responses . .	=370	Total of good social responses . .	=107
Total of anti-social responses . .	= 8	Total of anti-social responses . .	= 25

Significance of Results

The total results are obviously significant, showing a greater number of socially valuable responses and a smaller number of anti-social responses in the case of the experimental schools. Even if the very large difference in socially valuable responses in the classroom were entirely due to the traditions of freedom to talk in the one case and of quiet in the other, this cannot be true of the behaviour in the playground in which also a large difference (though not as large as in the classroom) is found. The difference in the number of anti-social responses is greater in the playground than in the classroom observations. It is quite evident that the children in the experimental schools were distinctly more friendly and co-operative towards each other than were the children in the control schools, and that quarrels were less frequent.

TEST X.   ARITHMETIC

Purpose of Test. To measure the relative attainment of the children in the experimental and control schools in arithmetic.

It was decided to give this test as late as possible in order to test the result of the whole year's work when the children were between six and seven. In the experimental schools very little teaching of arithmetic is given before the children reach the age of six. These schools do not aim at achieving a particular standard in formal arithmetic at six, but rather at sending the children on when they are seven to the Junior School with a simple but sure foundation of knowledge upon which the Junior teachers can build. It therefore seemed advisable to test the children just when they reached the age of seven. This meant giving the test in the autumn of 1939, and unfortunately the outbreak of war and the evacuation of the children made it very difficult to collect them. Full groups of twenty for each school could not be obtained, and a few children of a slightly older or younger age were included to make the groups larger. The children also could not be paired quite as accurately as for the tests given before the war.

Again, owing to the war, the test had to be given to children after a prolonged absence from school, so that the results will not represent the previous standard reached by the children in either type of school. Most of them had been out of school for three months, and those who were in school had been admitted for a very short time to schools with which they were unfamiliar.

The test was adapted from Dr. Schonell's *Diagnostic Arithmetic Tests.*[1]

Two forms of the written test were used to prevent copying.

The children wrote their answers in pencil on the forms provided. In this way slowness in writing was not such a handicap as it would have been had they copied out the sums.

Procedure for Tester. The tester sees that the children write their names on the space provided on the form.

She shows them the addition sheet, and says, 'Here are some sums for you to do. Some of them are quite easy. They are all adding sums. There is a place for you to write the answers.' (Showing the squares.) 'Begin here' (indicating the first sum), 'and work all down this side first' (pointing). 'See how many you can get right. If you can't do a sum, leave it and go on to the next.'

She allows five minutes. Then stops them and says, 'It doesn't matter if you haven't quite finished, but I want you to do these sums now' (showing the second column of harder addition sums). Allows five minutes. The tester walks round to see that the children follow the instructions, but gives no help with the sums. If a child finishes either column too soon he is told that he may work sums on the other column.

The subtraction sheet is given in the same way, except with the words, 'These are all "taking away" sums.' Then a break of about twenty minutes is given, and after that the reading test is taken. (See Test XII.) This takes four minutes.

Then Part II of the Number Test is taken. This consists of multiplication and division sums and problems. The problems are given orally and the children write the answers. If necessary, the tester prevents copying.

[1] Published by Oliver & Boyd.

Method of Scoring. In the sums on the four rules one mark was given for the simple equations and two marks for sums which contained a possibility of two errors in the answer. The problems were given one mark each.

Test X. *Significance of Results*

Schools   Marks for Arithmetic

Iₐ & ʙ $\dfrac{\text{D.}}{\text{A.D. diff.}} = 2\cdot3$ Against the experimental school

IIₐ & ʙ $\dfrac{\text{D.}}{\text{A.D. diff.}} = \cdot5$

IIIₐ & ʙ $\dfrac{\text{D.}}{\text{A.D. diff.}} = 5\cdot4$

IVₐ & ʙ $\dfrac{\text{D.}}{\text{A.D. diff.}} = \cdot37$

The results are therefore inconclusive. In Schools IIIₐ and IIIʙ, where the children are rather older than in the other pairs of schools, the results are significantly in favour of the experimental school. In Schools Iₐ and Iʙ, where the children are poorest and mentally youngest, they are against the experimental school by an amount which is fairly significant. In other schools there is no significant difference.

The results appear to indicate that in the case of the average seven-year-olds the difference in methods had not affected their proficiency in arithmetic. The extra time devoted to this subject by the control schools does not appear to have produced superior results by the time the children were seven-year-olds, though it may have done so in the case of children whose mental age was six.

TEST XI. WRITING

Purpose. To compare the standard of handwriting between the children in the experimental and in the control schools.

For the children aged six plus the results of Test Number I*b* in which the children had been asked to copy from a book were used.

The children were asked once to do their best writing, but after this nothing further was said on the subject, and no advice was given on posture. Except in School IVA the children were comfortably seated in their usual way for writing. In School IVA the room did not contain sufficient tables for the whole class to do written work at once, so that some children had to use chairs as tables, which may have been a handicap.

Points of Technique discovered in the First Year

This test was experimented with in order to gain practice in assessing the handwriting and to decide on a means for assessing it for the final tests.

At first the handwriting was marked on a six-point scale.

Class I. Awarded 5 marks. Very neat, even, and well spaced.
  ,, II. 4 marks. Neat and legible.
  ,, III. 3 marks. Legible, but not neat.
  ,, IV. 2 marks. Untidy or with several mistakes.
  ,, V. 1 mark. Very untidy, hardly legible.
Not classed. O. Illegible.

It was found, however, that assessors differed a good deal in their judgments, and even the results of the same assessor making two separate assessments of the same sets of writing were disappointingly unreliable. It was decided, therefore, to use the 'Metropolitan Handwriting Scale' for comparison, and it was found that results tended to be more reliable when marked on this scale than on one of merely verbal description. It was also decided to use three assessors in view of the difficulty of reaching a fair assessment.

The test was given to six-year-old children in six pairs of schools, three of which were marked on the original and three on the new system. In both cases in two out of the three pairs of schools the control schools were superior. In the fifth pair the results were equal, and in the sixth in favour of the experimental school.

Method of Assessment. The writing was examined by three independent assessors, who marked the work according to the 'Metropolitan Primary Handwriting Scale'.[1]

This scale sets out specimens of children's writing in a manuscript, and also in a cursive hand, and awards a mark to each specimen, the highest mark being 70 and the lowest 10. Assessors were asked to adhere to these marks or to give five marks for work which was between one class and another.

In assessing the writing, the instructions are to take into consideration general appearance, legibility, letter formation, uniformity of direction, and evenness of line and spacing. The work was assessed for quality. Speed was ignored in this assessment and marked separately for the number of letters written per minute.

In some cases the writing was so much of the type of that given in the scale that a decision was fairly easy, but in other cases, when the child's writing differed considerably from any of the writing in the scale, the task was more difficult. There were not, however, many cases of very wide divergence of opinion between the assessors, who were all teachers accustomed to seeing the writing of young children.

The correlation between the first two raters of the test in Schools IA and B was found to be ·9, and this is quite a representative set of the general difference in ratings.

This test was given earlier than the tests in reading and arithmetic, and it was intended to repeat it at the age of seven. The children in the experimental schools seldom began to learn writing much before the age of six, while the children in the control schools began at five, so that to give the test at six plus was not allowing long enough to test the experimental schools fairly.

[1] By Gertrude H. Hildreth, the Lincoln School, Teachers' College, Columbia University. Published by the World Book Company, Yonkers-on-Hudson, New York.

Owing to war-time difficulties, however, it was possible to test seven-year-olds in one pair of schools only. The results are appended after the six-year-old tests and show a striking improvement in the experimental school which has moved from being below the standard of the control school to being above it, both in the style and speed of writing.

The general slowness of the experimental groups in the six-year-old tests is almost certainly due to the unfamiliarity of the exercise, but the pair of schools tested later show that in this case it did not create any prolonged handicap.

Test XI (i).   Significance of Results

Schools	Assessments for Writing
Iᴀ & ʙ	Not significant
IIᴀ & ʙ	$\dfrac{\text{D.}}{\text{A.D. diff.}} = 2\cdot3$ Against the experimental school
IIIᴀ & ʙ	$\dfrac{\text{D.}}{\text{A.D. diff.}} = 5\cdot5$ Against the experimental school
IVᴀ & ʙ	Not significant
IIIᴀ & ʙ (at the age of 7+)	$\dfrac{\text{D.}}{\text{A.D. diff.}} = 2\cdot0$

It is evident that at the age of six plus such differences as exist are against the experimental schools, but the one pair re-tested at seven plus shows a difference in favour of the experimental school which is fairly significant.

These results indicate that the extra time and attention devoted to the practice of handwriting in the control schools has resulted in the superiority of the children's writing at the age of six plus over the writing of children of this age in the experimental schools. This superiority, however, was not maintained after the age of seven, in the pair of schools tested. (See Test XV.)

Test XI (ii). Speed of Writing

Schools   Rate. *Number of Letters per minute*

Ia & b $\dfrac{\text{D.}}{\text{A.D. diff.}} = 4\cdot2$ Against the experimental school

IIa & b $\dfrac{\text{D.}}{\text{A.D. diff.}} = 3\cdot8$ Against the experimental school

IIIa & b $\dfrac{\text{D.}}{\text{A.D. diff.}} = 2\cdot3$ Against the experimental school

IVa & b $\dfrac{\text{D.}}{\text{A.D. diff.}} = 0\cdot5$ Insignificant

IIIa & b
(re-tested $\dfrac{\text{D.}}{\text{A.D diff.}} = 4\cdot3$
at 7+)

It is again clear that such results as are significant are ever more against the experimental schools at the age of six plus, in the matter of speed, than the style of writing, but at seven plus in the one pair of schools tested it was even more significantly in favour of the experimental school.

TEST XII. READING

Purpose of Test. To measure the relative attainment of the children in the experimental and control schools in reading.

For the reasons given in Test X, it was considered advisable to test the children just on promotion to a Standard I class. Like Test X, it was given under the difficulties created by the war.

The *Detroit Word-Recognition Test*[1] was used. Owing to the kindness of Dr. Mary MacTaggart at St. Gabriel's College, London, the test was first tried with London children of the same age and found to be very satisfactory.

[1] By Eliza F. Oglesby, A.M. Published by the World Book Company, Yonkers-on-Hudson, 1925.

There are only two phrases likely to present difficulty to English children, 'A can of corn' and 'A boy eating corn', and in both types of school the intelligent children succeeded in recognizing them. The test is pleasant to administer because the children enjoy it and, since it contains familiar words from everyday life as well as rather short words, it is, like many tests of reading, applicable to children who have learnt to read by sentence methods as well as to those who have learnt by phonic methods. The test consists of drawing lines from words and phrases to their appropriate pictures. Two forms of equal difficulty are provided so that children cannot copy from their neighbours.

The procedure for the tester is given in the manual of directions supplied with the test, and was exactly followed.

The method of scoring is also carried out according to the directions given on page 4 of the manual of directions.

Test XII. Significance of Results

Schools	Marks for Reading	
I$_A$ & $_B$	$\dfrac{D.}{A.D.\ diff.} = 2\cdot8$	Fairly significant. Against the experimental school
II$_A$ & $_B$	$\dfrac{D.}{A.D.\ diff.} = 1\cdot1$	Not significant. Against the experimental school
III$_A$ & $_B$	$\dfrac{D.}{A.D.\ diff.} = 0\cdot5$	Not significant
IV$_A$ & $_B$	$\dfrac{D.}{A.D.\ diff.} = 0\cdot6$	Not significant

TEST XII

The slight tendency of the results to be against the experimental schools is gradually diminished and finally lost as the schools rise in the social district, and consequently in the children's mental age.

It again appears that although the extra time devoted to

reading in the control schools may show some favourable result at the age of six, such superiority over children educated less formally is not maintained when the children reach the age of seven. These results and those of Test X seem to indicate that neither system of Infant School education can claim to secure superiority in reading and arithmetic at the time when the children are seven years old.

FOOTNOTE TO CHAPTER IV

The outbreak of war in September 1939 had a very disturbing effect on my third year's work. Eight of the ten schools which I was then using for testing purposes were evacuated.

Many of the children remained at home, and I had to collect them individually by writing to, or calling on, the parents, and also by borrowing buildings in which to hold the tests, in the districts in which they lived.

I tested other children in the reception areas. This consumed much time in correspondence, first to discover where the children were, and later to obtain permission to give the tests. Giving the tests also took much longer than before, since not only were most of the children at a considerable distance from me, but the children from one school were often scattered in several villages. It was therefore impossible to carry out as many tests with the older children as I had previously planned. Moreover, although every effort was made to obtain the best possible conditions, and the courtesy of the Head teachers in the reception areas and of those responsible for church and community centre halls helped me very much in this work, still the conditions for testing were not as good as for the tests given during the first two years. The tests given under these less favourable conditions are those numbered X–XVI. Numbers I–IX were given under normal conditions, as were also the preparatory experimental tests carried out in the first year.

CHAPTER V

TESTS FOR CHILDREN AGED SEVEN AND EIGHT

General Remarks on the Tests for Children aged Seven plus and Eight plus. It was originally intended to carry the research further in two ways:

(i) By repeating (with some slight modifications) for children aged seven plus all the previous tests from IA to VII, and the observations of social behaviour. A written test was to be substituted for the oral in case of Tests I*b* and VI.

By this means it was hoped to measure the differences between the experimental and control groups, not only, as had already been done, during their final year in the Infant School, but also at the end of the Infant School period. The tests in reading and arithmetic were taken for the first time at that age.

(ii) By testing children aged eight plus from the one pair of schools available where there had been no change of Head Teacher in September 1936, and where the children had therefore had a consistent type of education from five to eight years of age. It was intended to modify the tests to bring them up to the capacity of eight-year-olds, but to test as widely as for the seven-year-olds, and to add a test in written composition.

When the war broke out, however, it quickly became evident that it would be impossible to cover the entire programme outlined above.

It was therefore decided (i) to give the reading and arithmetic tests to as many seven-year-old children as could possibly be collected, and (ii) to test the eight-year-olds from Schools IIIA and IIIB in reading, written composition, arithmetic, and free drawing. The free drawing was selected as being a test which might give some indication of whether the earlier superiority of the experimental children in a test requiring originality and creative power had been increased or lessened when they had entered on their life in the Junior School. The tests in reading and arithmetic were selected in order to see whether in the event of greater backwardness being found in the experimental school at the age of seven, this would have been overcome at eight. As it proved, the children in the experimental school actually did slightly better in these tests at seven plus, despite the relatively shorter period given to these subjects in the Infant School. It is, however, possible that the superiority was accounted for by the very unfortunate fact that so few younger children were available that the average age of the group is seven years six months instead of just seven as was intended. The average age of the control group is seven years two months, and a difference of four months at this age can make a considerable difference to skill in reading and arithmetic. On the other hand, the experimental school was evacuated and the children lost much schooling while the control school was not, so that actually the four months' advantage to the experimental school is very much less than it appears. The tests were given in late October and such children as had had any schooling at all in September and October had experienced a change of school and the disturbance of leaving home, whereas the control school had opened more or less normally in mid-September.

By February 1940, when the eight-year-old tests were given, the experimental group was seriously handicapped. School IIIA did not open until a few days before Christmas and few of the children had remained in the reception areas very long, so that many of them had had very little or no school education from midsummer to Christmas. Considering this handicap, it seemed scarcely worth attempting to test them at all, but since it was the only school which could be used, and since the disadvantage was to the experimental group, it appeared desirable to see whether they could hold their own at all against children whose school life had been scarcely interrupted. In arithmetic they could not do so, but in the other tests they did remarkably well. By waiting until the end of February it was hoped that they might by two months in school have regained much lost ground, but, owing to staffing problems occasioned by the evacuation, they were put in charge of three successive teachers during this time which created another severe handicap.

Preliminary Intelligence Test. It was first necessary to find a group intelligence test suitable for eight-year-old children. Since the main tests to be given involved reading and arithmetic, it was considered inadvisable to choose, as a basis for pairing the children, a group test requiring much of these attainments. Alexander's *Junior School Grading Test*[1] was chosen. The test is really intended to help in grading seven-year-old children on entering the Junior School, but it affords ample scope for testing eight-year-old children.

The children found the test difficult. There were a few children who had previously taken the Pintner-Cunningham Test, and who were tested again. In every case the score was lower when calculated by the Alexander Test, and the general level of I.Q. indicated by these tests is lower than that calculated by the Pintner-Cunningham Test, two years previously.

However, since there was no appreciable difference in favour of the children in the control schools (which would mean that they might be set against children whose real I.Q. was higher than theirs) the test has been used as a basis for forming the two groups for comparison. The children enjoyed the test despite the difficulty and they undoubtedly put forth effort.

TEST XIII.   ARITHMETIC (FOR EIGHT-YEAR-OLDS)

The test was based, as in the test for the seven-year-olds, on Dr. Schonell's *Diagnostic Arithmetic Tests*. Harder sums were selected and the problems given in written form. As before, the children were supplied with forms on which they wrote the answers only.

The test was tried with children not used as subjects who were given no time-limit, and it was found that the quickest

[1] *Junior School Grading Test.* W. P. Alexander, 1937. University of London Press.

children finished the first sheet in seventeen minutes and the smaller sheet in four minutes. It was decided to fix the time-limit as twenty minutes for the first sheet and seven minutes for the second.

Procedure for Tester. See that each child's name is written on his paper.

Say, 'Here are some sums for you to do. Some of them are quite easy. Write the answers on the papers.' (Show them where.) 'If you get to a sum you can't do, just leave it and go on to the next.' Allow twenty minutes. If a child does not know what to do the instructions may be repeated, but no other help may be given. Then give the small sheet, with the same words. Allow seven minutes.

In assessing this test only one mark was awarded for each sum. The maximum was therefore fifty-seven marks.

Test XIII . Significance of Result. (Arithmetic.)
School

IIIA & B $\dfrac{\text{D.}}{\text{A.D. diff.}} = 2$ (against the experimental school)

The result is against the experimental school by a fairly significant amount.

TEST XIV. READING (EIGHT-YEAR-OLDS)

The Haggerty Reading Examination, Sigma I,[1] was used. Dr. Mary MacTaggart kindly tried the test with London children and reported that she found it very satisfactory. There are very few words in this test which are used in America and not in England, and although the two words 'fall' and 'locate' on page 6 are examples of such words, failure to comprehend their meaning does not prevent the child from answering the questions asked.

The procedure given in the test booklet is followed precisely.

Test XIV. Significance. (Reading.) The difference between

[1] *Haggerty Reading Examination.* M. E. Haggerty and M. E. Noonan, 1929. Published by the World Book Company, Yonkers-on-Hudson.

the two sets of results is insignificant, which suggests that, had the experimental group not been handicapped, it might have proved superior.

TEST XV.   WRITTEN COMPOSITION (EIGHT-YEAR-OLD CHILDREN)

Purpose of the Test. To measure the relative ability of children in the two groups to express their ideas in written language.

The tester simply said, 'Can you think of a story of your own, about anything you like? I want you to make up a story of your own and then write it.'

In both cases the children started happily and without hesitation. Some children, however, especially in the control school, wrote stories which they had previously read or heard, instead of making up a story of their own. In the control school the class teacher insisted that only about 20 per cent of the children would be capable of making up an original story, and she strongly advised against repeating the words of the test, saying that the tester had 'made quite clear what was wanted, but that the children were incapable of telling an original story, and certainly could not write one'. The words were not therefore repeated in either school.

The writing was done in pencil, and no help was given with punctuation, spelling, or composition. The tester encouraged the children to work independently of her.

It was decided to assess the handwriting separately, using for this purpose the first twenty words written by each child. The tendency of young children to write less well as their ideas come quickly is a strong one, and it was considered a fairer test to base the assessment on work done while they were fresh. Otherwise a child who had many ideas and who wrote a long composition might appear a worse writer than a child who had very little to say.

It would, of course, have been possible to have given a piece of transcription for this test, but for eight-year-old children skill in transcription is less important than normal handwriting.

The 'Metropolitan Primary Handwriting Scale' was again used for assessment, as in Test XI, and again was marked by three independent assessors.

The composition was assessed independently of writing and punctuation, and nearly independently of spelling, although if the spelling were so poor that it made the composition very difficult to follow, it was considered in the assessment. For more detailed grading of the spelling and punctuation, however, separate assessments were made.

The assessors adhered closely to the following scale in making their classification:

Composition. Class I. (i) The story must be original, in the sense of not being merely re-told as it stands in a book or story with which the child is familiar. The idea may be taken from a book or film, but there must be elements in it which the child has composed for himself. (ii) It must be complete with a beginning and an ending, not suddenly broken off. (iii) The story must be conveyed clearly to the reader. (iv) There must be considerable fluency of ideas and expression. (v) There must be evidence of real ability to use words well.

Class II. (i) If the story is not original it must be re-told very well—with a standard equal to or approaching Class I in all other respects.

For original stories. (ii) The story must be complete. (iii) The story must be conveyed, although there may be some gaps and inadequate expressions. (iv) Fair fluency. (v) Fair ability with words, *or* (vi) An interesting story very well told, but rendered partially unintelligible by very bad spelling.

Class III. (i) If the story is not original it should be up to or not far short of, Class II standard.

If original. (ii) The story need not be complete, but should be partially clear and evidently intended for a story. (iii) More gaps are allowable, even if they make parts of the story incoherent, *or* (iv) A short not very interesting anecdote, *or* (v) Quite a good story rendered very difficult to read by bad spelling.

Class IV. Incomplete, broken-off story, difficult to understand owing to incoherence and poor wording, yet giving some intelligible sentences. At this standard no notice is taken of whether the story is original or not.

Class V. Quite incoherent.

The composition was marked by three assessors, two of whom, though accustomed to reading the writings of older people, had no connexion with the education of young children.

The punctuation and spelling were much more easily judged on an objective basis, so only two assessors were used, and their marks agreed in almost every case. In the rare cases of divergence of opinion a closer comparison of the work with the scale nearly always resulted in agreement. In the very few cases where there was still a difference of opinion the mark was given half-way between the two classes.

Scale for Assessing Spelling. Class I. Almost every word spelt correctly and hard words not avoided. A very small proportion of errors in difficult words only.

Class II. Most words correctly spelt, but more errors allowed than in Class I.

Class III. Easy words spelt correctly, but most harder words spelt wrongly, *or* some hard words spelt correctly, but a fairly large number of easy words misspelt.

Class IV. A great many mistakes even among the easy words.

Class V. Almost everything misspelt.

Scale for Assessing Punctuation. Class I. Punctuation almost correct. Full stops, commas, and inverted commas used where necessary. One or two omissions are allowable if at least three kinds of punctuation are correctly used.

Class II. Two kinds of stop correctly used with few omissions *or* use of the full stop only, provided it is used every time it is necessary and not incorrectly.

Class III. A few stops used correctly, but with a good many omissions or misuses of stops.

Class IV. Two stops only, used correctly, and a great many omissions and mistakes.

Class V. No punctuation, or nothing but a final full stop.

Test XV. Significance of Result

Schools

IIIA & B $\dfrac{\text{D.}}{\text{A.D. diff.}} = 2{\cdot}6$ (assessment for composition)

$\dfrac{\text{D.}}{\text{A.D. diff.}} = 4{\cdot}5$ (assessment for writing)

For spelling and punctuation the result is insignificant.

This result shows that, despite their interrupted education, the eight-year-old children in the experimental school have excelled over their controls, both in composition and in handwriting. It is interesting to connect this result with the tests in spoken language given nearly two years earlier, in several of which the experimental group was found to be superior. Neither of these tests have been taken with very large numbers of children, but there does appear to be an indication that the experimental methods have a favourable influence upon the ability to express ideas in words.

TEST XVI

This test in free drawing for seven- and eight-year-old children was the same in purpose and method of presentation as Test V (free drawing for six-year-olds). It was considered wiser with these older children not to standardize the materials, but to let each set of children use the type to which they were accustomed, except that the control group was supplied with better pastels and rather larger sheets of paper than those to which they were accustomed. With the greater attention to technique given by these older children, the imposition of quite unfamiliar materials was likely to prove a serious handicap. Assessors were, however, warned that they must discount the greater attractiveness of the experimental group media, and consider in making each assessment of a drawing done in pastel whether the same work done in paint would have been in a higher class, and, if so, place it higher. Every case of doubt about the medium causing the work to seem less attractive was given in favour of children in the control group.

There was no doubt in the minds of any of the assessors, who were again artists, that the difference in artistic power shown in their assessments is not due to the differences in media. Still less does the question of the media used affect the evidence of ideas, in a manner unfavourable to the control group.

The results in Test V (Schools IVA and B) where both media were used by two groups gives evidence on this point.

The artist assessors in this test found it less difficult than with the younger children's tests to come to a decision, and they were of the opinion that there was no need, at this age, to separate the questions of artistic merit and evidence of ideas. It was decided, therefore, to let them mark the pictures for artistic merit only and to let the evidence of ideas be marked by other assessors, educationalists whose chief interest in children's drawings lay in the ideas portrayed.

The experimental groups, both at seven and eight years old, were handicapped by evacuation and absence from school, but, as in the other tests, the handicap of the eight-year-old children was the more severe.

Test XVI.   Significance of Result

Schools	Assessment for Artistic Merit	Assessment for Ideas
IIIA & B at the age of seven	$\dfrac{\text{D.}}{\text{A.D. diff.}} = 4 \cdot 8$	$\dfrac{\text{D.}}{\text{A.D. diff.}} = 1 \cdot 2$
At the age of eight	$\dfrac{\text{D.}}{\text{A.D. diff.}} = 2 \cdot 8$	$\dfrac{\text{D.}}{\text{A.D. diff.}} = 2 \cdot 8$

The results are all in favour of the experimental schools, and very significant in the case of artistic merit for the seven-year-old group. They are also fairly significant in favour of the eight-year-olds in both respects. They are not significant in the case of ideas in the seven-year-old group. These marks may be affected by extra credit given to the control group to compensate for their use of pastel, which is actually not such a handicap as assessors are inclined to think, especially in the reproduction of ideas, in which it possibly has an advantage over paint with young children's work.

There is no doubt that in artistic work the children from the experimental schools were superior. The drawings were vivid and full of movement, and the colours used were much more interesting. There was also much greater variety of treatment. For instance, it was evident that certain children were beginning to experiment with perspective and they were interested in portraying such things as a house partially hidden by rising ground or an aeroplane coming straight towards one. The drawings were chiefly from first-hand observation. In the control school there was more conventional and symbolic representation of objects (suggestive of the work of younger children), and most of the subjects were illustrations of traditional fairy-tales.

Note on the Combining of Certain Tests on One Day

Some of the tests were given on the same day. Care was taken to see that experimental schools were tested in the same order and at the same time of day as the control school.

The tests that were taken on the same day were as follows:

Taken in the Afternoon

Test VIII followed by Test V. Interval for play, then Test III.

Test I*b* (which includes Test XI). Interval for play, then Test IV.

Test II*a*. Interval for play, then Test I*a*.

Test VI (Sub-tests (i)–(iv)), followed immediately by Test II*b* (all given individually).

Test VI (Sub-test (v)) was taken separately.

Both the above were taken on afternoons during which the children had been observed in connexion with Test IX.

Test XV. Interval for play, then Test XVI.

Test VII (Physical Training) was taken either in some pairs of schools at 2.20 p.m., or in others at 3.30 p.m. It is important that it is not taken immediately after the dinner or recreation intervals.

Taken in the Morning

Test X and XII (as described in the test procedure).
Test XIII, followed after an interval for play by Test XIV.

FURTHER WORK SINCE FIRST EDITION OF THIS BOOK

Miss Metcalfe Smith, M.A., in an unpublished research at Leeds University in which she investigated the development of number concepts, followed up some of the children used in my research and has stated that, at the age of nine years, she found that the children who had attended a formal type of Infant School were in no respect of their number work better than the children from the informal one, and that the latter were better in eleven out of fourteen aspects of number which she tested. These results varied in significance from 1·1 to 3·3 using the same formula as I used. Both in tackling problems and in straightforward division and subtraction sums the children from the informal school were superior to the others. She used eighty-two children (forty-one in each group) paired for age, intelligence, sex and social background. The children came from ten Infant Schools, six of which were formal and four informal, and at the time of her research were attending thirteen Junior Schools.

CHAPTER VI

GENERAL CONCLUSIONS

LET US now look at the facts revealed by the response of the children in these two types of schools to the tests given, and consider the bearings of these results on our own problems of teaching.

Tests Ia and Ib. The first of these are the tests for concentration. With regard to concentration on a subject of the child's own choice, it is quite evident that the danger that the children in the experimental schools might have lost the power of concentrating has not materialized. Moreover, in two out of the four pairs of schools tested, they concentrated better than their controls by a significant amount, and in the third pair the results also tended to be in this direction. In no case were they worse in this respect. The result suggests that the richer opportunities for first-hand experience, which is characteristic of the experimental schools, has not deterred but actually encouraged the growth of the capacity to concentrate. Norsworthy and Whitley state that 'The starting-point for habits of attention is in the sensory field. Ideas . . . become capable of holding the attention only as they are the outgrowth of experience in perceptual form'.[1]

With regard to the capacity to concentrate upon an uninteresting task which the children were asked to do with a good reason for doing it, it is again the case that not only is the experimental group no worse than the control group, but in three out of four pairs of schools it is better, in two cases by a very significant, and in one by a fairly significant amount. It might be objected that the idea of being asked to do an uninteresting task was more novel, and therefore more attractive to the experimental group, but in no case were the methods in use in the experimental schools so free, that the children had no experience at all in doing exercises in formal

[1] *The Psychology of Childhood.* Norsworthy and Whitley, 1937, p. 141.

work for the sake of practice. From the age of six the children in all the experimental schools had had a short period daily of practice work which they had not chosen, but which they were asked to do by the teacher. The motive suggested for this particular task was a new one to both groups of children. It is possible that it would make greater appeal to children whose social development was more advanced, and Test IX certainly indicates that this was the case in the experimental group, but at least these results may be said to indicate that the children in the experimental schools had not lost the power of concentrating on an uninteresting task for some ends other than their own.

This is an important point, since it is so frequently stated that children educated on the informal methods will only do what they like doing. As has already been stated, the 'experimental' children were not skilful at writing, and their progress tended to be slow and rather laborious. It is unlikely that they found the task very pleasurable.

Tests IIa and IIb. To turn to the question of the children's power of listening closely and of carrying out directions given to them, here again, in the test in which the children were asked to illustrate the passage read, the results show that in three pairs of schools out of four the experimental have excelled. Again, in two pairs of schools the results are significant, and in the third they are nearly so. In the fourth pair they are in favour of the control school, but by a quite insignificant amount. The capacity for giving close attention to the words of a teacher does not appear to have been impaired in these experimental schools by the education given. It is possible that the impression often given that the children are not learning to listen in schools where there is much play is caused by the general stir and conversation among the children which gives the onlooker the idea that they are not as attentive as the children in schools where there is more quiet. Actually it often astonishes visitors to see how quickly the children in a good school of the informal kind will stop their active play and listen attentively when the teacher has something to say to them.

The results of the test of questioning children individually upon a story they have heard are insignificant. It was probably a mistake to have selected this test from a battery of intelligence tests. The fact of its inclusion among such tests probably means that it is highly weighted with the quality of general intelligence, and that the equality of result between groups in which children were paired according to intelligence was therefore to be expected. It serves as another indication that the pairing by the Pintner-Cunningham Test was satisfactory.

The test does, however, show that children in the experimental group were not inferior in the capacity to attend closely as many formal teachers would expect to have been the case.

Test III. With regard to the question of tidiness in work, the results were insignificant in every case except one, in which the result was in favour of the experimental school. Interesting evidence that the capacity of young children to do neat work seems bound up with the question of maturation rather than of practice was given in the case of School IIA. The children in this school are younger than those in their control school, and therefore it was necessary in order to obtain equal age groups to test them three months later. During the first year this fact was not realized until working out the groups to be used for scoring this test, in which they had apparently done very badly. It was therefore determined to wait for three months and then to repeat the test. During the interval these children had no practice whatever in this type of work, but only general experience of using constructive and expressive materials in play. However, when tested again at the correct age, they easily equalled their controls, who were accustomed to regular practice in exercises of a similar kind to that given in this test.

Test IV. The test for ingenuity and inventiveness, and the power to express ideas which was given by asking the children to form pictures out of conventional shapes was, in all four pairs of schools, strikingly significant in favour of the experimental groups. The results of both this test and of the test for free drawing have been very consistently in favour of the experimental groups. There is now no doubt in my mind that the qualities required for this particular test are encouraged by education based on play much more than by formal methods, however good. I should like to see this test tried in a greater number of schools and followed up with older children. The capacity of the children to invent interesting and often beautiful forms out of the somewhat unpromising material supplied has been most striking in all the experimental schools. This fact seems to me an important one since the qualities of ingenuity, and still more of creative imagination on which success in this test seems largely to depend are qualities of such vital importance in life. I will quote again from the authors mentioned above, though, indeed, statements of considerable force and clarity are made by many other psychologists upon the subject of creative imagination.

Having pointed out that imagination, if it is to reach its highest development, must be given 'opportunity to develop and material to feed upon', Norsworthy and Whitley (page 237) go on to say, 'It (i.e. productive imagination) is one of the most precious abilities of the human race and should be developed and fostered by all means at the command of education. Upon the wealth and fertility of imaginative power man must depend for all the suggestions which will make this world other than it is.'

I regard the results of this test, and the one which follows it, together with the observations on social behaviour, as the most interesting outcome of this research.

Tests V and XVI. Here again, in the test of free drawing, creative imagination and the power of expressing ideas are required, but in a medium which is not so limited and circumscribed as in the above test.

In every case of the seven pairs of results obtained, the experimental school has been very significantly in advance of the control school except in the case of the eight-year-olds who had just previously lost five months of school life, and with it the opportunity to do very much creative work. Even there the results are fairly significantly in favour of this group. The paintings of these children actually reach a very high standard in many cases, but, as has been explained (see Test XIV), a good deal of compensation, possibly too much, was given to the control group for having to use pastel. It was unfortunate that the same materials could not be used by both classes.

For richness of ideas in the pictures, four pairs out of five of the six-year-old children showed a result significantly in favour of the experimental schools. In the remaining pair of six-year-old tests, and in the seven- and eight-year-old tests, the result, though in each case in favour of the experimental group, was not very significant; but in one pair (the eight-year-olds) it was nearly significant. The third assessor in the case of the seven- and eight-year-old children was perhaps again slightly over-anxious to compensate the control groups for their use of pastel, and in the matter of representing ideas, this was by far less necessary than in that of artistic merit. In fact, as the results of Schools IVA and IVB, who did the test in both media, rather seem to indicate, the use of pastel by young children may be more conducive to representing ideas than the use of paint, with its greater emotional appeal. The difference between the assessment for ideas was in favour of the experimental schools by a greater amount when pastel was used than when paint was, though it is true that there were four more children in the groups using pastel. The difference in artistic merit, however, is greater (again in favour of the experimental schools) when paint is used.

Drawing is, of course, a matter which might be greatly influenced by the teaching of art given by particular teachers. Very much less technique is taught in the experimental schools than in the control schools and such teaching as there is is given verbally and chiefly by encouragement of the child's own ideas, not by demonstration or the use of models. Much more actual teaching is given in the control schools, but less time is spent on creative activities, in general. On the other hand, every child in a control school gets regular experience of some kind in drawing, while in the experimental schools it is often possible for children who are not attracted by drawing to choose other activities.

There is no doubt that the personality of an artistic teacher has an influence on the work in art in her class, but it is unlikely that, in every pair of schools, the teacher in the experimental school would be more artistic than the one in the control school, and it certainly appears as if the greater freedom to play and express their own ideas, and the absence of formal art teaching in the experimental schools have had a favourable effect upon the children's work in art.

Test VI. The ability of the children in the experimental group to express themselves orally was superior by a significant amount in the tests of answering questions on differences between pictures and in the building of good sentences from certain words given.

In naming pictured objects and in defining words they were slightly superior, but not by significant amounts.

In spontaneous language they gave evidence of much greater fluency, better power of description, and had more to say about the picture-book shown.

It would have been desirable to test capacity in oral language much more widely and with greater numbers of children, but the time taken by individual testing and the detailed type of assessment necessary made it impossible to go further in this research. From the small numbers available, however, it appears that the practice, in the experimental schools, of encouraging spontaneous conversation, rather than conducting 'picture talks' and 'conversation lessons', has had a favourable effect. In no language test did the control group score above the experimental group.

Test VIII. The test for self-confidence and for confidence in a strange adult shows a result very favourable to the experimental schools, and could it have been carried out with larger numbers would probably have proved significant. As it is, it must be considered suggestive rather than conclusive.

In this connexion it is interesting to note that the ratings, in the test for physical training, of the children's attitude to a strange tester are all higher in the experimental schools than their controls.

Test IX. The observations made on six periods of classroom or playground activity for each child yield results which are very favourable to the experimental group and, as with Test IV, I should very much like to follow it up with larger numbers of children. It is one of the tests in which the results are most consistent and very interesting. The observers had no idea of differences in the school régime, nor of why they were asked to do the work, beyond knowing that it was an investigation of the social behaviour of the children. It is not possible, therefore, that their records are biased by any preconceived ideas of the advantages of one type of school over another. Although there are certain omissions in the records, the characteristically friendly and co-operative relationship of the experimental group comes out clearly, both in the records used for this study, and in the large number that were rejected either for inadequate recording or because the children did not pair closely enough for age and intelligence with those in the other group. The numbers, though small (twenty-nine children in each type of school), are closely paired. The analysis of Test IX throws, I think, some light on the question of whether the freedom given in the experimental schools has made the children self-centred and inconsiderate of others. Points particularly relevant, and in which the experimental group scored very well, are the following:

1. Willingness to invite or accept another child into a group.

2. Acquiescing in another child's suggestion.

3. Contributing willingly to the work of a group, even in some cases by accepting a less attractive role.

4. Helping or advising another child constructively.

5. Taking a friendly interest in another child's occupation.

TESTS ON SUBJECTS OF THE INFANT SCHOOL CURRICULUM

Test VIII. In the exercises for physical training two of the experimental schools scored higher for energy in the opening exercises, and all four experimental schools for adaptability in the same exercises. Two schools by a significant, and one by an almost significant amount, scored higher on their ability to follow out the rather complex instructions in exercise (vi). All four scored successfully by a significant amount in their quickness at getting out apparatus and starting work without quarrelling or fuss, and all again scored significantly higher in their relationship with, and response to, the stranger who gave the tests.

The control groups tended to do better in the exercise (which it was afterwards decided to discard) of alternately bowling to the skittles and fielding for the child opposite. As previously explained, this made an unsatisfactory game and was very difficult to assess. However, for unquestioning obedience in following the rules given, the control groups did better than the experimental groups, who tended to change the rule.

The other results are not significant. Some of the control schools, as well as some of the experimental schools, took a keen interest in physical training; it was not, I think, the case that the teaching of this subject was appreciably better in one type of school than in the other. In neither type of school did the children appear to be weaker in muscular control, but the exercise was undoubtedly rather easy. The problem of finding exercises hard enough, and not too hard, is one which needed further exploration, and which the scattering of the children by evacuation unfortunately prevented. The idea of taking such a test emerged as the result of the kind co-operation of my colleague, Miss Stephen, which was not available until the second year, so that this test suffered from lack of experimental work in the first year.

It is, of course, not claimed that single exercises for such qualities as 'adaptability', as understood in physical training, can test adaptability as a general trait in personality. The test was intended to explore the children's capacity in physical work, using exercises which required different kinds of qualities and skill.

Tests X and XIII. The test in arithmetic, given at the age of seven, showed insignificant results except in the case of Schools IIIA and B, where the children were older than in the other pairs of schools.

In School IA very few children could be collected for the test. They had been out of school for many weeks and came from very poor homes. School IB was slightly more mixed, and many of the children who came were from the better homes. On the other hand, the test in this group was disturbed by a 'gang' of boys who tried to break into the hall in which they were being tested. In spite of the interruption, this control school did better than its experimental school by a fairly significant amount.

As has been explained elsewhere, all the tests from number X onwards were given after an interrupted education, and they represent what the children had retained after the interruption rather than what they would probably have known at the end of the summer term. There were signs that the control groups had learnt more of the four rules than had the experimental groups. They got the easier sums in division right, for example, while some of the experimental schools had obviously not begun to teach division to the children tested. Any great advantage that there may have been does not, however, appear to have been maintained after such a long interruption. An interesting feature of this test is that the children in the experimental schools made more attempts to do sums that were too hard for them, especially in solving the problems. The children in the control schools were more inclined to leave blanks for such answers and to become restless when they could not do the sums. This possibly shows wisdom on their part, but seems another indication that the children in experimental schools were not averse from making efforts.

In the test for eight-year-olds the experimental school was much more severely handicapped than its control. The results are against them, moderately significant amount.

It certainly appears that had their education proceeded normally they would have equalled their controls. Arithmetic is perhaps the subject of all others in which lack of practice is the most severe handicap.

Tests XI and XV (i). The first assessments of writing were made very early when the children in the experimental schools had been learning only a short time. The results for standard of writing are inconclusive. In two cases the differences are insignificant, in one the result is significantly against, and in another fairly significantly in favour of the experimental school.

The speed, however, is in every case against the experimental group, though in one case by an insignificant and in another only a fairly significant amount.

At seven plus, in the one pair of schools tested, the experimental group excelled in both quality and speed by a significant amount, and at eight plus the superiority in quality was still maintained in spite of the handicap mentioned above. Speed was not tested again, since the writing was assessed from a test in composition, not from continuous copying.

This school was the one which was the most significantly lower than its control, when the children were tested at six plus. The results indicate that so far as these children were concerned early retardation did not continue to form a handicap.

Tests XII and XIV. At seven plus, in reading as in arithmetic, the experimental school was inferior to its control in the case of Schools IA and B (the poorest schools, in which the children were mentally youngest). The other results are not significant.

At eight plus the result is in favour of the experimental school by a fairly significant amount, which had they been less handicapped, might well have been more significant.

Test XV (ii). In written composition, which was only taken with the groups aged eight plus, the result is again in favour of the experimental school by a fairly significant amount. In spelling and punctuation the results are approximately the same. Considering the prolonged absence from school of the experimental group the result is a clear indication of their ability to express ideas in this way. Some of their stories were vivid and original.

SUMMARY OF RESULTS

(a) *Tests in which the experimental schools were distinctly superior.*

1. Assembling material ingeniously to make interesting pictures.

2. Free drawing and painting and expressing imaginative ideas through drawing.

3. Answering specific questions asked, making good sentences, and expressing themselves spontaneously in words.

4. Showing a friendly and responsive attitude to a strange adult.

5. Good social behaviour towards other children.

6. Writing quickly and neatly at seven and eight years old.[1]

7. Concentration on a task of their own choice.

(b) *Tests in which the experimental schools certainly tend to be superior, but the results are not uniformly in their favour in all tests, or else were not carried out under very satisfactory conditions.*

8. Concentration on a task which they are asked to do, but which is not immediately interesting.

9. Listening to and illustrating a passage read to them.

10. Performing certain exercises in physical training.

11. Performing a task which needs self-confidence.

12. Writing compositions at eight years old.[1]

(c) *Those in which there is no significant difference between the two groups.*

1. Answering questions in a story read to them.

2. Carrying out a task in handwork neatly and carefully.

3. Defining words, naming pictured objects.

4. Performing certain exercises in physical training.

5. Working the answers to simple sums in arithmetic.
        (Both at seven and eight years old).

6. Reading (at seven and at eight years old).

7. Spelling and punctuating (at eight years old).[1]

(d) *Those in which the control groups are superior.*

1. Writing quickly and neatly (at six years old).

2. Keeping to rather unattractive rules in a game which involved following a teacher's rules for co-operating with others.

---

[1] These tests are taken in one pair of schools only and cannot therefore be considered as of equal importance to the tests which were given in four or more pairs of schools.

GENERAL BEARINGS OF RESULTS

The results of this research have proved unexpected to me in two particular directions.

First, I had imagined that the amount of extra time spent on the teaching of reading, writing, and arithmetic would have resulted in a striking superiority of the control groups in these subjects at the age of just seven, though I was not anticipating that this superiority would necessarily be maintained very far into the Junior School. It is, of course, possible that had the tests been given without the interruption caused by the war, the children in the control schools might have scored better results. The control schools were no more handicapped than the experimental by this interruption. They were, in fact, less so, since two of the control schools (IIB and IIIB) were in a neutral area and opened after a long break, but in their own building with their own staff. It appears, therefore, that even if the children had scored higher results by being tested when fresh from school, their knowledge would not have been of the kind which could last long without revision.

Secondly, I had not anticipated that the tests in which the experimental schools proved to be superior would have shown such clear results. Although I had thought it possible that some results might have been in their favour, I imagined that most of the differences would have been more difficult to measure and would probably not have appeared at so early a stage in a form capable of scoring results in test situations.

Some of the results of tests in which the experimental schools were successful seem to touch on matters of great importance and of far-reaching consequence in the development of children, and it seems likely that a wider investigation of this whole question, based upon greater numbers of schools and children, would produce many significant results which might have a favourable influence on the education given in Infant Schools.

It certainly appears probable that such an investigation would prove a support to teachers who believe in allowing the young child to learn by means of his natural activities, and who postpone formal instruction until the child's growth makes him ready and eager for it. It might also afford real relief from strain for both teachers and children in those schools where it is now considered the teacher's duty to aim at early precocity in formal attainments.

If we look back to the pictures of the two typical schools with which this book opens, we recall the eager buzz of conversation between the children and the informal chatting which went on between teacher and child in School 'A', and we remember the easy informal way in which the children moved about the school while engaged in many purposeful activities. It is impossible not to connect this picture with the fact that the children in this type of school were found to excel those in schools of the 'B' type in the power to express ideas by means of words. We find, too, that there was more helpfulness, more willingness to accept other children's ideas, and to co-operate for common purposes, more friendliness between the children themselves and between children and adults, and greater willingness to volunteer for a task needing self-confidence.

The apparently greater concentration of attention in School 'B' is found to be deceptive, since it was the children from schools of the 'A' type who were found to have the greater power of concentration.

The varied activities and free play with many materials which is characteristic of School 'A' has resulted in far more than the happiness of the children. It was the children from the 'A' type of school who excelled in the very important qualities of ingenuity, adaptability, and richness of creative imagination.

Nor was it found that the dangers anticipated by so many teachers had actually materialized as a result of the freedom allowed by Schools 'A'. These children were actually more willing than were those from Schools 'B' to spend time on an uninteresting task when asked to do this for a good reason. They attended more closely to detailed instructions given by a teacher than did the children in the 'B' type of school. They equalled them in neatness and care when performing a task which required these qualities. In the actual subjects of the school curriculum, the children from Schools 'A' excelled in drawing, in creative handwork, and in several of the tests in language and in physical training. In the other subjects tested, they equalled the children who had been educated more formally, with the sole exception of handwriting at the age of six plus. There was some indication that this inferiority at six plus might also have been shown in reading and arithmetic, had these subjects been tested, but at seven plus there was no appreciable difference in the standard of reading, writing, or arithmetic between the two types of school. If this be so, then superiority at six plus is of no importance to the child. Unfortunately in some districts the children are promoted to Junior Schools at little more than six plus. Such a system is likely to lead to forcing in the Infant School and to be detrimental to the child's best interests, because the teacher will feel that the results of her work in the Infant School will be judged on the attainments in reading, writing, and arithmetic of children who are six plus or only just seven years of age.

Assuming that further investigation confirms the results of this research, it would seem that the formal type of Infant School does not justify all the effort and anxiety which it demands from both teachers and children, nor the sacrifice of so many other valuable things on the altar of early skill in reading, writing, and arithmetic. It is true that the informal type of education as practised in School 'A' requires more thought and greater ingenuity on the part of the teacher, since it involves an intelligent following up of the child's spontaneous activities rather than a prearranged formal scheme.

It brings, however, far less strain and anxiety in her relationships with the children. Although the teachers in schools of the 'A' type are perhaps working harder than some of the more formal teachers, they generally appear to be happier and more natural in their bearing. Some teachers, it is true, have become so accustomed to formal methods and formal discipline that they would find it almost impossible to change. Most teachers, however, if they became convinced of its greater value, would be ready and eager to follow a system of education based on greater freedom for the child to learn in his own ways.

Few teachers would feel any regret at bidding farewell to the 'conversation lesson', or the formal handwork lesson designed to give 'hand and eye training'. Still less would they regret the long laborious hours in which they have tried to instil the arts of reading, writing, and arithmetic into restless five-year-olds. As for the children—children who are so often called 'lazy' when all they desire is to be more active, 'inattentive' when their eager curiosity is impelling their attention towards the world of real things and first-hand experiences— there can be no doubt of the relief to them. To some teachers the happiness of children is a sufficient sign of their well-being, but other teachers want assurance that they are gaining something besides happiness. It is to offer some evidence that such assurance could be forthcoming that I have written this book.

Further research is greatly needed. If this book suggests to other people that some of the tests are worth following up or that better tests should be devised, it would be desirable to carry out tests with a larger number of schools, and particularly with eight-year-old children. (My own investigation was so seriously curtailed in this respect.) It would also be of great value to test children of nine and ten years old, so that the long-distance effects of their Infant School education might be ascertained.

The Junior Schools. Few Junior Elementary Schools to-day can claim that their education is based on the natural interests and ways of learning of children in the middle years. There is, however, a growing discontent on the part of all progressive teachers about the handicaps imposed by bad buildings and large classes, above all, by what amounts to a competitive examination at the end of the Junior School course, an examination which regards the child's ability in formal English and arithmetic as the most important criterion for determining the whole course of his later education.

It is greatly to be hoped that reforms in the educational

system of the country will bring better days for the Junior Schools. It may be that in the future a large number of Junior Schools, freed from the burden of the Junior Scholarship examination, will begin to work on lines of greater freedom. The type of education given in Infant School 'A' would then have a logical sequel, and a research carried further on the lines of the present investigation would be a valuable means of assessing the results of the newer methods.

In the meantime it may well be found that even the formal type of Junior School benefits in the long run from an informal type of Infant School education for the children who eventually come into it. Many Junior School teachers to-day are quite aware that children who come from Infant Schools such as School 'A' have greater initiative, more independent habits of work, and greater enthusiasm for learning; that they understand more of what they read and contribute more actively to the work of the class than do the children from the 'B' type of school.

Other Junior School teachers seem to care for little but formal efficiency in reading, writing, and arithmetic and constantly complain that the children's standard in these subjects is not higher. It is commonly these teachers who lament the loudest that the formal work done by the children who come up from Infant Schools is mechanical and unintelligent, that they cannot apply their arithmetic to the solution of problems, and that they read without comprehension of meaning. Such teachers do not realize that this is the inevitable consequence of the Infant School teacher's attempts to bring the children to a standard which is beyond their natural capacity. It often happens that the Junior School teacher has little idea of what is going on in the Infant School from which her children come. I have often been told (sometimes quite tolerantly) by Junior School teachers that Infant School education nowadays is 'one long play time', whereas in fact the particular Infant Schools from which these teachers draw their children deny their children all opportunity for play in school after they are five years old. They actually devote the major part of their time and energy to 'the three "R's" ' in the very hope of satisfying the demands of the Junior School. If the Junior School teacher realized the true situation he would often be the first to see that his interests would be far better served by reducing this pressure and by encouraging a more active learning in play for his pupils to be.

Many Junior Schools do co-operate well with their Infant Schools, but on the whole it is still true that a greater understanding and greater continuity between the Infant and Junior Schools is needed. If they worked more closely together they would surely see that their interests are in fact the same.

The results of this research offer evidence that modern methods in the Infant School encourage qualities which the Junior School teacher finds valuable, as they are found to be in actual life. Few Junior School teachers will not feel satisfaction in teaching a class of children who show initiative and imagination who are articulate and capable of concentration, are friendly and responsive to adults and to other children, capable of co-operating happily with each other, and of tackling unfamiliar tasks with confidence. The Junior School in which such qualities are considered to be undesirable is not only a very depressing place, but, fortunately, extremely rare. The principle laid down in the Board of Education's *Primary School Report* is now widely accepted: 'The schools whose first intention was to teach the children how to read have been compelled to broaden their aims until it might now be said that they have to teach the children how to live.' The results of the research which I have described in this book offer evidence that the teacher of Junior School children has nothing to fear but everything to gain from Infant School methods which make use of the free activities and spontaneous interests of the children.

FURTHER ACKNOWLEDGMENTS

I

Work which was of Direct Use in Testing the Children.[1]

(*a*) The intelligence tests of Rudolph Pintner, Grace Cunningham, and W. P. Alexander.

(*b*) The work of Dorothy Van Alstyne and Mary Gutteridge in measuring the attention span of young children to different types of play material.

(*c*) The revised scale of intelligence tests of Lewis Terman and Maud Merrill for the tests of vocabulary, of sentence building, and of memory for a story.

(*d*) The diagnostic tests in arithmetic of F. J. Schonell, from which, with his advice, I adapted my own.

(*e*) The tests in reading of E. F. Oglesby and M. E. Haggerty.

(*f*) The method of assessing the handwriting of primary school children devised by G. H. Hildreth.

II

For indirect suggestions which have helped both in the choice of tests and in finding methods of assessing them, I am also indebted to many workers in the field of investigation in child psychology. The chief of these are:

(*a*) Ruth Griffiths (42) for her studies on the imagination of five-year-old children. These suggested rich possibilities in investigating the capacity of young children to express their imaginative ideas in drawing and in composing original stories.

(*b*) Cyril Burt for his tests on the scholastic attainments of older children and for general information on calculating the significance of the results of tests.

[1] The full titles and publishers of the works mentioned have been included in Section III of the Bibliography. Where I have referred to books in other sections of the Bibliography I have given the reference number.

(c) Katherine Bridges (39) for her scale of recording and studying the social and anti-social behaviour of pre-school children in a normal school environment. (She also suggests that the free play period is the most fruitful time for observing the social contacts.)

(d) Margaret Barker for pointing out that the social contacts in a playground differ from those in a playroom, which confirmed my decision to observe the children in both situations. Among many valuable studies based upon observation of the social behaviour of pre-school children I have found these particularly suggestive.

(e) Dorothy Van Alstyne and Louisa Farwell for studies on the reactions of children to certain types of play material. These suggested (i) that the range of materials provided in the experimental schools was adequate and contained the most important materials for the development of young children through their play; (ii) that certain qualities are likely to be encouraged by such play.

(f) S. R. Laycock for his idea of testing adaptability to new situations, although his methods with boys of eleven and twelve were not suitable to be applied to young children.

(g) The New York Bureau of Analysis (pp. 75–111) for the 'Four-Detail Drawing Test'. Although intended for children of eleven years of age, the authors suggest that success in such a test depends on 'the attention given and upon auditory visual and retentive memory'. This suggested that my use of a similar type of test with children of six and a half was suitable for testing the above qualities.

(h) Dr. Susan Isaacs (31) for comments on the use of rating scales given in her suggestions for record-keeping by Infant School teachers, published by the Wiltshire Education Committee.

III

Much general advice on methods of testing children and precautions to be taken, and also on general principles affecting the question of reliable and unreliable research methods has been gained from the following writers:

(*a*) Jones and Burks: *Personality Development in Childhood*.
(*b*) Goodenough and Anderson: *Experimental Child Study*.
(*c*) Bühler and Hetzer: *Testing Children's Development*.
(*d*) Stoddard and Wellman: *Child Psychology*.
(*e*) Cyril Burt: *Mental and Scholastic Tests*.
(*f*) H. R. Hamley: *The Testing of Intelligence*.

The above books contain useful reviews of the different methods most generally used in studying young children, and of the advantages and dangers of using them and the factors which must be taken into consideration before arriving at conclusions. Jones and Burks particularly give detailed criticisms on the validity of many researches, some of which are claimed on inadequate grounds to have established conclusions.

Bühler and Hetzer's book is particularly valuable for advice on the technique of testing young children. It deals chiefly with children under six, and makes the somewhat startling statement that, 'The six-year-old is a subject on whose co-operation we may count with as much certainty as on that of an adult.' Much of the technique which is suggested for younger children I have found to be applicable to six-year-olds also.

BIBLIOGRAPHY

Section I (*a*). Books on the general value of play.

1. Cook, Caldwell: *The Play Way.* 1917. Heinemann.
2. Curtis, H. C.: *Education through Play.* 1915. The Macmillan Company.
3. Dewey, J.: *The School and the Child.* 1906. Blackie.
4. Dewey, J.: *Schools of Tomorrow.* 1915. E. P. Dutton & Co., New York.
5. Froebel, Frederick: *Education of Man.* 1887. D. Appleton & Co.
6. Gardner, D.: *The Children's Play Centre.* 1937. Methuen.
7. Groos, K.: *The Play of Man.* 1901. D. Appleton & Co.
8. Hall, Stanley: *Aspects of Child Life and Education.* 1907. Ginn.
9. Johnson, G. E.: *Education by Play and Games.* 1907. Ginn & Co.
10. Lee, J.: *Play in Education.* 1915. The Macmillan Co., New York.
11. Lowenfeld, M.: *Play in Childhood.* 1935. Gollancz.
12. May, D. E.: Article on Play in the *New Era Magazine.* 1937.
13. Nunn, Sir Percy: *Education. Its Data and First Principles.* Revised in 1930. Edward Arnold.
14. Rainwater, G. E.: *The Play Movement in the United States.* 1922. University of Chicago.
15. Reaney, M. J.: *The Place of Play in Education.* 1926. Methuen.
16. Wood, W.: *Children's Play.* 1915. Kegan Paul.

Section I (*b*). Books which describe systems of modern education for young children.

17. Board of Education: *Nursery and Infant Schools.* 1933. H.M. Stationery Office.
18. Board of Education: *The Primary School.* 1931. H.M. Stationery Office.
19. Boyce, E. R.: *Play in the Infant School.* 1938. Methuen.
20. Catty, N.: *Modern Education of Young Children.* 1933. Methuen.
21. Slight, J. P.: *Living with our Children.* 1933. Grant Educational Co.
22. Staff of the Lincoln School of Teachers' College, Columbia University: *Curriculum Making in an Elementary School.* 1927. Ginn & Co.
23. Stevens, A.: *The Activities Curriculum in the Primary Grades.* 1931. Heath.

24. Sturt, M.: *Education of Children under Seven*. 1932. Routledge.

Section II (a). Books which include useful data on the normal characteristics of children from six to nine years of age.

25. Board of Education reports on *Nursery and Infant Schools* and
26. *The Primary School*. Chapter III and Appendix III referred to in Section I (*b*).
27. Bühler, C.: *From Birth to Maturity*. 1935. Kegan Paul.
28. Bühler, K.: *The Mental Development of the Child*. 1933. Kegan Paul.
29. Curti, M. W.: *Child Psychology*. 1930. Longmans Green & Co.
30. Goodenough, F.: *Developmental Psychology*. 1934. New York—Appleton.
31. Hamley, H. R., and Others: *The Educational Guidance of the School Child*. 1937. Evans Bros.
32. Isaacs, Susan: *Intellectual Growth in Young Children*. 1930. Routledge.
33. Isaacs, Susan: *The Children we Teach*. 1932. University of London Press.
34. Kenwrick, E. & M.: *The Child from Five to Ten*. 1930. Kegan Paul.
35. Lane, Homer: *Talks to Parents and Teachers*. 1928. Allen and Unwin.
36. Norsworthy, N., and Whitley, M.J.: *Psychology of Childhood*. 1937. The Macmillan Co., New York.
37. Rasmussen, V.: *The Primary School Child*. 1929. Gyldendal.
38. Strang, R.: *An Introduction to Child Study*. 1936. The Macmillan Company.

Section II (b). A few studies of Pre-school Children and some general books on Child Psychology and Education which throw light on subjects with which this research is concerned.

39. Bridges, K.: *Social and Emotional Development of the Pre-School Child*. 1931. Kegan Paul.
40. Bott, H. M.: *Personality Development in Young Children*. 1934. University of Toronto Press.
41. Gesell, A.: *Mental Growth of the Pre-School Child*. 1925. Macmillan.
42. Griffiths, R.: *Imagination in Early Childhood*. 1935. Kegan Paul.
43. Isaacs, Susan: *The Nursery Years*. 1929. Routledge.
44. Koffka, K.: *The Growth of the Mind*. 1925. Kegan Paul.

45. Löwenfeld, V.: *The Nature of Creative Activity.* 1939. Kegan Paul.
46. Murphy, Lois Barclay: *Social Behaviour and Child Personality.* 1937. Columbia University Press.
47. Piaget, J.: *Language and Thought of the Child.* 1926. Harcourt Brace.
48. Stern, W.: *Psychology of Early Childhood.* Revised 1930. Allen & Unwin.
49. Waddle, C. W.: *Introduction to Child Psychology.* 1920. Harrap.
50. Wagoner, L. C.: *Development of Learning in Young Children.* 1933. McGraw Hill Book Co., Inc.

Section III. Books which contain principles of testing children or which suggest methods of research allied to those used in this study.

51. Alexander, W. P.: *Junior School Grading Test.* 1937. University of London Pre
52. Ballard, P. B.: *Group Tests of Intelligence.* 1928. Hodder & Stoughton.
53. Ballard, P. B.: *Mental Tests.* First published 1926. Last revised 1930. Hodder & Stoughton.
54. Barker, M.: *A technique for studying the social and material activities of young children.* 1930. Child Development Monograph. Teachers' College, Columbia University.
55. Bronner, A. F., Healy, Lowe & Shimberg: *A Manual of Individual Mental Tests and Testing.* 1928. Little, Brown & Co., Boston.
56. Bühler, C., & Hetzer, H.: *Testing Children's Development.* 1935. Allen & Unwin.
57. Burt, Cyril: *Mental and Scholastic Tests.* First published 1921. Last published 1933. London County Council.
58. Cunningham, B. V.: *The Prognostic Value of a Primary Group Test.* 1923. Teachers' College, Columbia University.
59. Farwell, L.: *Observations of Play Activities in a Nursery School.* 1928. Genetic Psych. Monographs.
60. Farwell, L.: *Reactions of Kindergarten, First and Second Grade Children to constructive play materials.* 1930. Genetic Psych. Monograph. Vol. VIII, Nos. 5 and 6.
61. Goodenough, F. L., & Anderson, J.E.: *Experimental Child Study.* 1931. The Century Company.
62. Gutteridge, M. V.: *The Duration of Attention in Young Children.* 1935. Melbourne University Press.
63. Haggerty, M. E., & Noonan, M. E.: *Haggerty reading examination.* Sigma I. 1920. Yonkers-on-Hudson. World Book Co.

64. Hamley, H. R.: *The Testing of Intelligence*. 1935. Evans Bros.
65. Hildreth, G. H.: *Metropolitan Primary Cursive Handwriting Scale*. 1933. Yonkers-on-Hudson. World Book Co.
66. Jones, M. C., & Burks, B. S.: *Personality Development in Childhood*. 1936. National Research Council, Washington.
67. Knight, R.: *Intelligence and Intelligence Tests*. 1933. Methuen.
68. Laycock, S. R.: *Adaptability to New Situations*. 1929. Baltimore, Warwick & York, Inc.
69. Lehman & Witty: *The Psychology of Play Activities*. 1927. A. S. Branes & Co., New York.
70. Oglesby, E. F.: *Detroit Word Recognition Test*. 1925. Yonkers-on-Hudson, World Book Co.
71. Pintner, R., & Cunningham, B. V.: *The Pintner-Cunningham Primary Mental Test*. 1923. Yonkers-on-Hudson, World Book Co.
72. Pintner, R.: *The Pintner-Cunningham Primary Test*. 1927. Journal of Educational Psychology.
73. Schonell, F. J.: *Diagnostic Arithmetic*. 1938. Oliver & Boyd.
74. Stoddard, G. D. & Wellman, B. L.: *Child Psychology*. 1934. The Macmillan Co.
75. Terman, L. M., & Merrill, M.A.: *Measuring Intelligence*. 1937. Harrap.
76. Terman, L.: *The Measurement of Intelligence*. First published 1916. Last published 1932. Harrap.
77. Van Alstyne, D.: *Play Behaviour and Choice of Play Materials*. 1932. University of Chicago Press.
78. Wynn, Jones Ll.: *Introduction to the Theory and Practice of Psychology*. 1939. Macmillan.